The Legat Story

By
Nadine Nicolaeva Legat

Cadmus Publishing
www.cadmuspublishing.com

INTRODUCTION

By Anna Aragno

It's not everyone's good fortune to have been schooled in one's chosen art form by a great teacher in an idyllic Kentish setting designed to maximize immersion and concentration in one's training. But it was mine. Along with an international group of like-minded eager young dancers I was to become one of the chosen students of Madame Nadejda Nicolaeva Legat, the author of this extraordinary autobiography of an extraordinary life. I learned this in the summer of 1956 after my first personal encounter with 'Madame' at my audition in London. As I entered the studio, shaking with nerves, at the piano sat the small but infinitely majestic frame of the famed teacher of Russian Ballet who, while playing her own accompaniment, observed my every movement as she steered the audition. Impossible to describe my excitement on learning that I had been accepted. My first big dream having now come true, I would thenceforth put myself in her hands, throwing myself completely into the Legat experience with results that shaped my character, values, and habits, honing body and mind in ways that have lasted a lifetime.

We learn through her own words how Madame was herself shaped by her great teacher and husband Nicolas Legat, a master pedagogue of the Maryinsky Imperial School in St. Petersburg. He, in turn, was trained and influenced by the famous Swedish and Italian ballet masters C.Johannsen and E.Cecchetti, before going on to form the finest and most famous dancers of his era. Legat was renowned and revered in Russia. After the revolution, and once in exile, he continued to teach a new generation of premier dancers throughout the capitals of Europe, ultimately settling in London. Madame transmitted this exclusive legacy through her own teaching of his method making us, her fortunate students, the beneficiaries of this élite balletic lineage. Only later, when I myself was dancing in Moscow and visiting the Vaganova School in Leningrad, did I fully grasp the importance and purity of the prestigious origins of this heritage. Here, in the pages of this engrossing history, I was introduced to Nadejda Nicolaeva *before* she became 'Madame', as she was becoming the great personage she would be to me. And through her own words I've had the privilege of connecting her younger self with mine, her student, meeting her anew, as it were, in a way that completes my admiration for the whole arc of her life.

Ballet attracts those whose passion for dancing obliterates everything else: it has to, since ballet training must start early in order to shape and accustom the body to the strain of its strict form. This training develops muscles of body and mind habituating both to a daily diet of technical and artistic effort. The rigors of a discipline born of love for an art form that demands the highest ideals of physical form, performed *effortlessly*, requires strenuous daily exercise in "Class", a communal ritual bordering on the sacred that begins at the outset and lasts the duration of the dancing life. We know each other on sight, a breed apart, those for whom dancing is life itself. From the youngest age I knew that this was the artistic family to which I belonged. Reading young Nadejda's story, her persistent, passionate commitment to dancing-- anywhere, wherever, at whatever cost-- made me realize that she was kin before I ever met her and that she recognized immediately those of us who were born ballerinas, just as she was.

Her life story interweaves with the history of Russian ballet at the time of its fortuitous export to the West often through the tragic vicissitudes of two world wars and the dislocating effect of the 1917 Bolshevik revolution. Nadiejda's generation lived through tumultuous times of shifting social hierarchies imposing terrible losses, separations, and dramatic change. Yet Russian leadership, whatever the ideology, seems to have consistently valued its artists, leaving them apart from the political turmoil, continuing to employ their contributions as though implicitly understanding that the Russian *"duschă"*, the soul of its people, needed the arts. Though stripped of the gilded insignia of Imperial patronage and now performing to audiences of common folk who had never set foot in a theater before, performances went on, all artists maintaining their highest standards. Dancers are ever dancers and though the revolution sliced into their lives, forcing an exodus from the cream of Russian ballet and pedagogy, it arrived in Europe to nourish a new generation of Russifed dancers that went on to form the heart of western ballet companies and their repertoires. The influx of superb artists at that time enhanced western culture infusing all the arts with creativity and new forms. Nadejda, we learn, travelled to the capitals of Europe with Nicholas, dancing everywhere: setting up studios in Venice, Paris, London, Monte Carlo; touring with Diaghilev, quarreling with Diaghilev; forming new groups, and indefatigably relocating from studio to studio in order to continue providing a "place" for dancers to take "Class" where the standards of classical ballet technique were preserved at the highest levels.

Although she does not enter into the details of her childhood, we learn that Nadejda Nicolaeva De Briger was one of four siblings born to a well to do family in the St. Petersburg of Imperial Russia. As admiral and head of the Imperial Naval Academy her Father's family would have been included in the court-life of the Tsar and Tsarina along with the entourage of Russian nobility. Nadiejda's passion for dancing and her early admission to the Maryinsky Ballet School would not have been particularly favored by her family but her willful independent spirit must have tested her parents even more when, expressing misgivings about her courtship with her teacher Nicholas Legat, twenty six years her senior, and disapproving of a marriage, she promptly eloped and married secretly! This kind of frolic is not surprising once we are introduced to the light-hearted, high-spirited, comedic, and *infinitely* talented Nicholas Gregorovich Legat, already a veteran performer and premier ballet Pedagogue at the Maryinsky! He was not only a strong and brilliant dancer and an accomplished choreographer, he also played the violin and piano, was a master caricaturist given to hilarious impromptu imitations of anyone who caught his eye, a great mime and an even greater teacher, who, it is said, received standing ovations from an audience that included the Tsar on the twenty fifth anniversary of his tenure as maître of Russian ballet. Among the list of legendary ballet dancers he produced are Karsavina, Nijinsky (with whom he had a special enduring rapport) Ksheshinskaya, Fokine, Oboukhov, Preobrajenskaya, Nemchinova, Danilova, Doubrovska, Vladimirov, Egorova, Balanchine, Lifar, Kyacsht, and of a subsequent generation, there was Markova, Dolin, Ninette de Valois, M. Rambert, the latter two founders of famous British ballet companies. Those influenced indirectly through teachers who studied with him include the *entire* roster of famous dancers of the Sadlers Wells, and of Madame's students among many others, Moirer Shearer stands out, a generation or two before mine.

Nadejda was passionately devoted to, and deeply appreciative of, her teacher and husband. Her very different more reflective, contemplative temperament, enabled her to enjoy Kolia's gregarious, insouciant nature, and benefit from his jovial optimism, especially through their hardest times. Yet it explains why she, and not he, wrote and finished the book they had worked on together. They were complementary; and while he was her senior in years he was not her superior. Devotion to a common art form and the utmost mutual respect made them a perfect match. Just as he knew he would carry the mantle of his great teacher Johannsen, Nadejda knew that one day she would continue her husband's teachings. But first she must dance! Her story revolves around the many tours that she and Nicholas embarked on; the different roles she danced; the theatres in which they appeared; the companies they joined and left and those they themselves formed; and the many studios they again and again installed where Nicholas and Nadejda Legat continued the rigorous perfectionist tradition from which they came. Of course, the tumultuous world events of their time, and especially their country, intruded into the smooth course of their artistic aspirations but never enough to stop the dancers dancing or the teachers teaching. Throughout Madame recounts the argumentative, capricious yet *always* flamboyant, ballet-world intrigues; the often tragic vicissitudes of lengthy separations from her daughter and family; the privations caused by inadequate food, warmth, and money, and the constant anxiety and fear, and lack of freedom, with the same level-handed perfect English prose that singles her out among émigrés. On the other hand, there were also sumptuous opening night parties, trips to Italy and the south of France, wine, close friends, and always, the glamour and magic of the Ballet. She tells her story straightforwardly, pragmatically, without sentimental fluff or sensational self-pity. And what a story it is!

Because this autobiography reads like an historical ballet novel, I would not anticipate too many details of its content. But a word about the writing: although, as mentioned, her lucid mind and pragmatism comes through, we also learn of her deep emotions, strong family attachments, loyalties, friendships, her intense longing for the past, her spiritual and intellectually searching nature, and her incredible openness to novelty and experimentation! Throughout her narrative we follow Nadiejda's inquisitive, probing intellect that questioned and sought ways to expand her awareness and understanding along psychological, philosophical, and spiritual dimensions. These traits led her to seek out Ouspensky and Gurdjeiff in his monastic seclusion where she observed dervish dances and experimented with trance states. We learn of her sense of humor and profound observational acuity, her appreciation of her beloved Kolya's genius and congenial fun-loving temperament. We hear of her seriousness too, the repeated trips to Gurdjievs sanctuary; her philosophical readings and taking up the practice of Yoga; her trials with cocaine and, in Algiers, even hashish!! All of these in her belief that the ultimate human achievement lay in mental mastery of the body, resulting in a lifelong quest to push towards this potential. This was no timid lady! She was to break with the strict classical tradition, and even her husband's taste, by introducing acrobatic style lifts into pas de deux, and to all these, her habits and traditions we, her students, were indoctrinated too. I, for one, have never abandoned the daily Yoga practice she instilled in us.

In this regard I remember a rather terrible day when a group of us senior girls, all dressed up in summer hats and white lace gloves, packed into the back of the minibus driven by Nan, Madame's daughter. We were heading to Lydya Kyacsht's funeral in London, when the drive-mechanism malfunctioned and we toppled to the left down a river bank, rolling over dramatically several times to land upside down in the river... Apparently I was the only one in the back aware of what was happening, who saw, and then felt, us pounding down and that on finally landing I was the only one conscious enough to scramble out of the broken windows and haul out anyone I could into the bloody river. Many were very badly injured requiring surgery, but not me, a fact that greatly distressed me as I felt guilty for coming away with just a few tiny scratches. As we all lay in the local hospital ward with Madame all bandaged up in a bed right in the middle, she said, "Girls, you see, Anna was not hurt because she does Yoga proper-ly" belying her deep belief in the power of mind over body! I knew that it was really because of my position in the minibus and because I had braced myself for the terrible impact. But I continue to do Yoga anyway!

After Nicholas' death in 1937 she was left to run the studio classes and face the war, alone. As she always did, she made the best of it, and when time came for the evacuation from London, she left for Mersey Is-land with her eighty-year-old Mother and a bunch of children. As she kept taking in more and more peo-ple, larger premises had to be found, this time in Bea-consfield, a little Buckinghamshire village. Here, in the most makeshift wartime circumstances of this "First House", where the dining room doubled up as class-room, studio, and dormitory, and where she and her aged mother selflessly cooked, cleaned, fed, nursed, tutored and trained their charges, the British Bal-let Boarding school, modeled on the Maryinsky, was born. At war's end, four and a half years later, predict-ably, still larger premises had to be found. And it is here, in the magnificent property by the lake in Royal Tunbridge Wells, that I come into the story!

My mother and I visited the Legat boarding school by attending the annual summer garden party of 1956 in the lovely grounds of the main house in Tunbridge Wells. I was certain from the moment I set foot in that wonderful house that this was where I wanted to be. As Madame writes "All day long the old house echoed to the sound of dancing feet, the music of pianos, and voices counting 'and one..and two.. and .'" and of children running up and down the stairs, to and from the 'cottage' the younger children's sleeping quarters. For anyone who wanted only to dance, this was the place; all classrooms were transformed into dressing rooms, each desk outfitted with a mirror and make up box; hair pieces and costumes draped the chairs and hung from doors; tights, point shoes, character shoes, and leotards, lay strewn around the sunny rooms with large bay windows looking out onto a spectacular view of the lake. This was magic! a ballet school materialized seemingly out of my dreams; the fit between this place and me was perfect. After acceptance there were fittings on Bond Street for special uniforms with capes and hats patterned on the Maryinsky traditions and after sad goodbyes to family and childhood were done, there began the core educative experience that was to shape my life. More than anything or anyone else, the Legat years laid formative foundations that have enabled me to accomplish what I have and, most importantly, that made me who I am today. They did this by providing an environment in which the highest standards of excellence not only in dance but in all the arts and education were implicit; where dedication and effort were the norm and hard work in striving to meet these standards was recognized and rewarded. In reading Madame's story, it is clear that this passionate spirit of tireless striving was the spirit in which the great Russian dancers and teachers approached their art. What Madame instilled in us was a continuation of traditions handed down from generation to generation. Not just a physical discipline and technique, but a way of being in life.

During my stay Madame increased emphasis on academic study importing top level teachers from Trinity College and Oxford. By demanding equally high standards in academic work Legat encouraged budding dancers to exercise their minds insisting that body and brain work together. A curriculum that included music, art, literature, history, mathematics, and languages, opened many doors while simultaneously succeeding in pushing every one of us to potentials that were always being stretched a little further. By offering exposure to national competitions, visits to museums, cultural events, and performing poetry and piano recitals, we became culturally aware and grew accustomed to the rigors of dependability. I feel so privileged to have acquired a love of form and discipline through the daily practice of artistic activities I lived in an atmosphere where devotion and values to live by were transmitted through the study of *ballet as education*, in its broadest sense.

At the heart of the "Legat" experience was Madame herself; indefatigable, authoritative, a great teacher of remarkable dignity, with reserves of infinite strength and wisdom. She simultaneously imposed the rigor of the Russian school with the technical and methodological innovations of her legendary husband. The exigencies of daily ballet class were formidable, increasing in difficulty as one went on, always ending with sixteen entrechats sixes and as many fouèttès as one could do!! I remember the exhilarating exhaustion that pushed one to compete with *oneself* every day. And then there was Madame's singular presence: Who could forget the hush that settled around us as she entered the studio for the morning class; with her tiny frame and limping gait, announcing what tragedies may befall a dancers body, or how she accompanied our training by playing the piano as she taught, inspiring, correcting and grading, all at the same time! And how she single-handedly was able to revive, rehearse and stage, three act ballets like Raymonda, in which I was the principle, in the first production ever performed in the West. Only retrospectively can one fully appreciate the scope of her accomplishments. Suffice it to say that by her discipline, demeanor and inner fortitude, exemplified in her insistence that we all be initiated into the daily practice of Yoga, she was, for me, the model of what a woman can become. She created a school where artistic talents flourished as we garnered a reputation for winning all the top awards at the annual Hastings Dance Festival. At the time I arrived there was quite a roster of teachers, including Lydia Kyacsht, Valentine Prorwitsch, Madame De Villiers, Miss Weguelin, Mr. and Mrs. De Briger for music and piano, Mr. Donovan, the headmaster, Dr Vickers the Oxford don, and the incomparable Mr. Eling, our wonderful accompanist. We were a colorful bunch, an international gathering of young dancing flesh, all joined by a collective passion for ballet that was exhilarating and kept us going from early morning to night. We worked hard, but I was amply rewarded; dancing Giselle at age thirteen the London Times reviewed our school performance with admiration and praise, naming me a child prodigy.

And what a wonderful time we had as well! Running back and forth from the "Cottage" or the "Braes", down by the lake and to the apple orchard...I remember in autumn picking the juiciest green apples by the bushel and storing them under the beds... to be eaten at midnight feasts! I can still picture Madame's mysterious private rooms on the second floor of the main building, looking out over the lake, rooms I still dream of. And then, later on during my time, there was yet another move, this time to a truly magnificent Queen Anne mansion named "Finchcocks", near the village of Goudhurst, in Kent. This huge multiple story manor, with its opulent oak-paneled entrance hall, its regal main stairway (which we didn't use) lined with Nichola's brilliant caricatures, its stately rose garden and grounds, it's beautiful frescoed studio and stables converted into music studios, is where I spent hours practicing ballet combinations, playing the piano, and studying for my GCE's. I remember the ample kitchen and Nan in it, cooking for the whole school! I even remember the menus. The second floor, off bounds for the most part, devoted to Madame's and the head-master's quarters, although I was invited to cut the cat's fresh liver and help prepare hors d'oeuvres for special Saturday meetings. I realize now that this was the time when Madame must have been writing her story, probably at night. She slept but a few hours, we were told,

And then, inevitably, came my last Garden Party. I danced the role of Colombine to Schumann's delightful music, and the pas de deux from the last act of Coppelia. A few days later, as the car that was taking me away wound slowly through the fields down the long Finchcocks driveway, I recall looking back, through a torrential flood of tears, at Mr. Donovan, Nan, and Madame, standing in the great doorway, waving me goodbye as I set out into my journey, an image that brings tears to my eyes, even now. How many times and for how many years did I continue to dream that I was returning to my beloved school! I left Legat with the *complete* classical ballet repertoire already learned and up my sleeve, ready to dance anywhere

In April of 1963, after a period at La Sorbonne and in the ballet studios in Paris, I flew to Moscow where I had won a cultural exchange program to apprentice as a young soloist with the Bolshoi. After only a few weeks I was dancing on the Bolshoi and Kremlin Stages with such legends as Fadeyechev and Ulanova in the wings, attending Messerer's and Semionova's classes and receiving hours of coaching at the Bolshoi, coincidentally also by Smaltzoff, mentioned in the autobiography.

Later, in New York, I found my way to classes with Madame Pereyeslavic and Alicia Markova, then Director of the Metropolitan Opera ballet and under Dame Alicia's auspices began my professional life. So, from Kent to Moscow to New York, the chain continued... With my husband and our six-month old infant, Natascia, I travelled to visit Madame in her last abode. Although she had lost the power of speech, now I could speak to her in Russian, hoping that it would make her happy and as proud of me as I was of her.

In this introduction to her story, it is fitting to include, in her own words, her deepest principles and goals as a teacher: In a prefatory note to her book 'Ballet Education' (1947) in which she expresses her desire to pass on her knowledge and experience to future generations inspiring an "insatiable desire for achievement," she also expounds on her creative vision for the "new artist," cataloging the attributes with which this artist would be equipped. As I move through my life, I realize that this vision, transmitted to me in youth in her teaching, was internalized first as a guide, and now as my ideal.

The "new artist", she writes, would have:

"... abundant knowledge, be broad-minded and idealistically ambitious; would search for new forms and expressions enveloping all the other arts and sciences within his own art; would raise him/herself and the spectators towards the Ideal; would set an example of generosity, encouragement, happiness, constructive criticism and fair judgment. With these qualities he/she will be liberated from negative emotions. Through dancing he/she will have learned the art of perfect control, will have mastered the art of observation, and will have attuned his/her body and soul to a state of perfect harmony. This artist will be eager to make effort, will conquer tiredness, will control emotion and banish fears". (p. xxiii paraphrased)

It is impossible not to marvel at such a vision or to *not* pay tribute to the person whose story this is. Were it only for the balletic time frame, Nadiejda's life story is riveting. But for those of us who knew her as "Madame", to have met Nadejda and Kolia, and to have known how she and her Mother gave of themselves selflessly to the children they took on during the war years, is a privilege indeed. These were extraordinary people. The Legat legacy lives within me and all her students; it has steered me, as she herself was steered, to successes as well as through valleys of despair and hardship. I am incredibly proud to say I went "Legat", and after you have entered the world of her story, you will better understand why.

Anna Aragno
New York, November 2020

Nadine Nicolaeva and Nicolas Legat

CHAPTER ONE

I was eleven when I first danced for Nicolas Legat. Wearing the traditional long bodice of white satin and a brief tutu, pink tights and shoes. I performed the steps for which the Maestro asked. His blue eyes watched me closely to the end. Then he nodded.

"You have very beautiful legs", he said gravely. I blushed with shy pleasure. Legat was twenty-six years my senior, principal soloist to his Majesty the Tsar of Russia, Ballet master and Professor at the Imperial School of St. Petersburg. How could I have imagined then that he would one day be my husband?

From early childhood my family was sure I would dance – for I was always up on my toes and never walked across a room. Once, when we had all been to a ballet performance at the Maryinsky theatre, my mother said only half in jest: "Perhaps we shall see Nadia dance there someday. If she is not as pretty as her sisters, she has more grace".

My Father

My father, Alexander de Briger, was an officer in the Russian navy, but at no time that I remember was he actually at sea. On marriage he gave up the life to which he was devoted and settled down to teach at the Naval College in St. Petersburg. My mother's family – which belonged to the deposed Obrenovic dynasty of Serbia – fled to Austria when she was a child, afterwards establishing a home in Russia. While she was still in her teens, my mother's fine singing voice won her the scholarship yearly presented by the Grand Duke Nicolas. This entitled her to prolonged study at the Conservatoire but, abandoning this promising career, she preferred to devote herself to her husband, later, to the children.

There were four of us; my sisters, Xenia and Olga, my brother Vladimir and me. Thin and small, my hair dark and unmanageable, I envied the appearance of my sister Olga whose hair fell in long blonde ringlets. I longed to distinguish myself in some way, and at night put myself to sleep with dreams of success and glory, sometimes grasping the bars of my bed and shaking them fiercely in inarticulate desire.

We girls learned dancing from a visiting teacher who was a member of the celebrated corps de ballet attached to the Imperial State Company. The steps came easily to me, but I was not strong and often missed classes through illness.

The main building of the Naval College faced the Neva River, and in my early days we lived in the west wing. In the entrance hall of our flat were models of frigates and clippers, presided over by a huge stuffed bear that stood in the corner, holding a tray for visiting cards. In the courtyard beneath our rear windows, boys and young men in black uniforms with white-and-gold shoulder straps marched and drilled daily. Later my father was made Assistant-Director of the College and we moved to the east wing. This flat was partly furnished when we took over and in one of the rooms, a silver-faced icon stood on a white piano.

The previous owners having denied all knowledge of it, my mother, who was devout, thought it a good omen. During the revolution, when danger threatened, she prayed all the time to this icon and felt her belief in its powers justified by her delivery. Each year on Boxing Day, a party for officers' children was held at the Naval College. We loved these occasions. The great hall with its fine ceiling suspended uniquely by heavy chains from above, was gay with the sound of music and childish laughter. My sisters and I wore fluffy tutus and danced to entertain the other guests. Afterwards we waltzed with the tall officers, clasping them round the knees as they bent over us. "My fiancé" I would call my favourite, gazing up at him proudly. When the

Nicolas Legat

evening was over the men carried us home in their arms, and we were asleep almost before we reached our rooms.

After Christmas there was Easter to look forward to. Families and friends went off to church together, to hold lighted candles and kiss each other three times. "Christ is risen!" we exclaimed joyfully. Then home again to eat paske – a rich creamy cheesecake – with koulitch pastry coloured with saffron and flavoured with almonds and raisins. My mother served tea in tall glasses; pale amber liquid poured from the teapot that sat above the great shining silver samovar, the centre of every Russian home. Many artists, writers, and dancers visited our flat. Among the latter was Nicolas Legat. I saw him dance at the Maryinsky in many ballets, partnering the famous ballerina Matilda Kshesinskaya, and others. To me he had two separate entities, one quite elderly by my youthful standards, the other a Prince Charming who wore a wig on the stage and danced every role to perfection. Off stage he was unassuming, a man of the utmost courtesy and gentleness. His eyes were a clear sky-blue, his mouth thin-lipped – with a humorous quirk at the corners. Though his hair thinned early, he always looked much younger than his years.

The Legats were connected with the Imperial theatres of St. Petersburg and Moscow for more than a century. Gustave Legat was a professor and Nicolas, his son, inherited his position from Christian Johannsen, thought by some to be the greatest teacher of them all. Neither Johannsen nor Marius Petipa – the famous ballet-master and producer – was born in Russia, though both adopted Russian nationality. Petipa was a Frenchman, Johannsen a Swede. Also, of Swedish birth was Gustav Legat, though his wife was Russian. Gustav trained his two sons – Nicolas and Serge – to be perfectionists like himself and in his book, "Ballet

Russe" Nicolas tells some almost incredible stories of his father's devotion to his art.

Serge Legat

Marius Petipa

М. М. ПЕТИПА.   M. PETIPA.

Marie Petipa

"The hardest worker I ever knew was my father", he wrote. "He was astonishingly strong. He was able to lift his leg in a developpe with a boy sitting on his foot. Another achievement was to carry a glass full of water steadily balanced on the inside of his heel with his leg raised in a developpe of the second position". *

(* *"Ballet Russe" by Nicolas Legat. Translated by Sir Paul Dukes, K.B.E., and published by Methuen*)

Nicholas, in his turn, had little mercy on his pupils during a lesson. Subsequently, when I was in his class, I often saw him rub his hands in glee as the sweat ran down our faces.

GUSTAV LEGAT TEACHING HIS TWO SONS NICOLAS AND SERGE

"Ah, now you are working!" he would say. "When my brother and I worked with my father, he saw to it that there was no need to sprinkle the floor. We sprayed it ourselves!" Like his father, Nicolas played the violin in the earlier days of his teaching. He walked up and down, plucking the strings with his fingers pizzicato fashion, and if a pupil exasperated him, he would sometimes reach out and administer correction with his bow. "Once I broke my bow on a pupil who afterwards became famous", he told our class, his face wearing the look of almost boyish mischief, which was typical. "She argued with me about her pirouettes. Later she apologised, but it was too late. I had then no bow!" Both as a dancer and as a teacher Nicolas was a vital part of the Imperial Ballet, indeed, he was one of its creators. When Enrico Cecchetti came to Russia in 1886 Nicholas saw him dance and was, as he put it, "Staggered" by the Italian's astonishing virtuosity. From that moment, Nicolas and Serge Legat, with a few of their contemporaries, set themselves to learn the Italian "tricks".

To these they added that superior grace and logic for which the Russian school has always been famous. The star ballerina of that time was Matilda Kschsinskya. She struggled to acquire from Cecchetti the technique of Legnani's famous thirty-two fouettes. Neither he nor Legnani, the Italian ballerina, seemed

Nicolas and Serge self-caricature

able to help her.

She began working with Nicolas alone, and when at last she mastered the feat, Legat received a gold cigarette case and a note of grateful thanks from the distinguished personage who was Madame Kschsinskya's friend and patron.

Nicolas and his younger brother were both good at drawing. They became recognised cartoonists and made caricatures in watercolours of almost all the famous ballet personalities of the day. When Stravinsky, father of Igor, urged them to publish these, they were made into a book. A copy bound in white leather and containing ninety-four cartoons, was accepted by the Tsar. Most of our possessions were confiscated during the revolution, and others abandoned when my husband and I left Russia together in 1922, but later, in England, we met Laurent Novikoff who still had one of the albums. He kindly allowed the cartoons to be reproduced and the prints, which now line the walls of my dancing school in Kent, were on display at the Diaghilev exhibition in London. The originals are, I believe, still in the Bakrushkin Museum at Moscow.

The death of Serge Legat at the age of twenty-five was a great sorrow to Nicolas. Serge was highly imaginative and temperamental. He conceived a hopeless infatuation for the daughter of Marius Petipa, a woman many years older than himself, and was found dead one day on the floor of his room, a razor in his hand.

Enrico Cecchetti

М. Ф. КШЕСИНСКАЯ.   M. KCHÉCINSKAJA.

Matilda Kschsinskya

My mother used to tell me that she watched the long funeral procession pass beneath the windows of the Naval College; Serge was a fine dancer and a popular personality.

It was Nicolas who first realised the dancing potential of Vaslav Nijinsky. When Nijinsky was brought to the Imperial school by his mother, the other examiners were not impressed. The boy seemed to them awkward and of a poor physique. Nicolas, however, was struck by Nijinsky's well- formed thigh muscles and asked him to do some jumps. Everyone was astonished by his high leaping and Legat, who as master of the senior classes had the last word in selection, declared: "We must have this boy. I believe he will make a fine dancer!"

Perhaps because of this early championship there developed an unusually close understanding between Nijinsky and Nicolas. Vaslav, so reserved with many, was at his best with his master and followed his advice with almost slavish obedience. He copied Legat's device of practising with weights attached to his waist and ankles; the idea being that a dancer, eventually released from such burdens, would feel able to jump inches higher.

Later, I too, followed this example, the only woman, as far as I know, to do so.

When the tragedy of mental illness put an end of Nijinsky's brilliant career, Nicolas was greatly distressed. Many years afterwards when he and I, together, visited

Nijinsky in Switzerland, Vaslav showed signs that he at least recognised his "Maestro".

In 1947, when Romola Nijinsky, his wife, succeeded at last in bringing Vaslav to England, I went alone to see him – as I shall tell later....

The members of the Imperial Ballet Company of Russia belonged to the State; or rather, they were the Tsar's servants. They were trained for eight years without charge and in return were expected to continue loyally with the Company. Most of them were agreeable to this arrangement, but during the long holidays, which lasted from May to September, dancers were glad to make extra money touring the Provinces or accepting engagements abroad. When

Vaslac Nijinsky

Serge Diaghilev conceived the idea of taking a ballet company to Paris he had little difficult in persuading others to join him in the venture.

Diaghilev was at one time attached to the Directorate of the Maryinsky Theatre, but owing to various misunderstandings, he received his dismissal. In 1906, he was presenting exhibitions of paintings in Paris; in 1907, he turned his attention to concerts, in 1909 to ballet.

He made ambitious plans. The Grand-Duke Vladimir, uncle to the Tsar, was his patron and promised not only a subsidy from the Imperial Treasury, but also the loan of scenery and costumes from the Maryinsky theatre. But the Grand Duke died, and Diaghilev ran into difficulties which only a determined person could have overcome. Overcome them he did, and the experiment prospered, as everyone now knows.

It was as a day-pupil that I first joined the Imperial School, the building was three-storied with large square windows and a frontage stretching almost the length of the street. On the ground floor were the offices; the second housed the girl pupils and the third the boys. On each level were dancing rooms with sloping floors that matched exactly the gradients of the theatre stages.

The girls dressed in dark blue frocks with pinafores over them; black for day-pupils and white for the boarders. The boys had black uniforms with high collars on which was embroidered the silver lyre. Dancers being trained for the Maryinsky could receive at the same time their general education, but in those days my parents had no thought of my dancing professionally. I shared a governess and tutors with my brother and sisters. At the Imperial school discipline was strict, the pupils took their dancing seriously, but like most young people found ways of eluding rules and amusing themselves at each other's expense.

Visits to the theatre were occasional and much-cherished treats. We were taken there in the Court carriages; elegant vehicles resplendent with the Imperial crest on shining green paint. The footmen and coachmen wore scarlet coats with capes, and black cocked hats.

During the performance we were kept under close supervision, but I think there was rarely any trouble. We loved this world of the theatre - our chosen world. I used to sit forward in my seat, imagining myself in the various roles, and when the performance came to an end, I was dazed and drugged with vicarious success. Sometimes the students had the honour of appearing on the stage among the ballet crowds, or in simple walk-on parts, but with only this, I knew I should never be content.

Several years before this the Tsar had withdrawn from the Winter Palace and now lived more usually at Tsarskoe Selo, the great palace built by Rastrelli for the Empress Catherine. I remember going there. Olga and I danced at a concert and afterwards the Tsarina kissed us and presented us each with a little brooch.

There were plenty of people in St. Petersburg however to keep going the gaiety of Court life. The vast Winter Palace was the scene of frequent grand occasions. On one side the Palace looked out onto the Square, big enough to hold a regiment and flanked by the longest crescent in the world. On the other side it faced the Neva river. Within the building was a fantastic gathering of huge, richly furnished rooms and galleries, classic pillars and marble staircases.

I use the past tense because that era, if not the buildings, is gone. The revolutionary Government, in 1917, moved from St. Petersburg to Moscow, which had previously been the capital. I have been told by people who have revisited the old city, that it has now an air of decay and neglect, and that the façade of the Winter Palace is a strange greenish-brown, and peasants clump up and down the marble staircases to gaze at the relics of bygone glory. I was a witness to that glory. Occasionally the young people of the Imperial School were summoned to a performance at Court. The long ballroom glittered with light from the many glass chandeliers. Jewels flashed, enhancing the beauty of the women's gowns, men wore splendid and elaborate uniforms with rows of medals. The scene was one to dazzle any youngster's eyes, but as soon as we began to dance, everything else was forgotten. Only our best was good enough for such an important occasion.

I threw myself into the work of the Imperial School with devoted enthusiasm. I loved it. I did not care how long the hours were, or how hard I had to work, if only I could improve. My love for ballet has always contained something spiritual, an almost religious fervour. In later years, when others commented on my single mindedness, I would explain: "The stage is my temple, dancing my prayers".

In the late summer of my first year at the Imperial School, however, my dancing received a serious setback. There was an epidemic of diphtheria in the city.

All the de Briger children caught it, but I was the most seriously ill. It was December before I was well enough to be propped up on pillows and encouraged to take an interest in the Christmas preparations.

Christmas in our household was always in the best tradition. A great tree was brought in from the miniature forest that sprouted annually in the Gostinvy Dvor, a nearby square where the shops were built around a centre court under an arcade of stone columns. The tree was set up in the centre of the hall and hung with tinsel and glittering decorations. Each branch carried some gift; for the girls, cardboard boxes shaped like Swiss chalets and filled with bonbons, for the boys, knives, tops, or whistles. There were huge crackers containing whole outfits in coloured paper and presents for every member of our large household. On Christmas Day, my father played a march on the piano, and everyone danced around the tree, stopping at last for the distribution of gifts.

This particular year, no children from outside could be invited, in case of infection. But some of the teachers from the College looked in, and the family and a few close friends determined to make it as gay as occasion as was possible.

I lay on a bed in a downstairs room with the door open, gazing out at the glittering tree. My father played the piano, and everyone pranced as gaily as usual. But the circle was small, and the chain of hands could not be kept intact. As the merrymakers chased after each other in a spirited attempt to keep going, no one but myself saw the huge tree sway; it had come loose in the pot. Though I tried to warn them, my weak voice would not carry.

As the great tree toppled and crashed on to the dancers, I hid my face in my hands, and then fainted. No one was hurt but when at last they were able to bring me back to consciousness I could not move, and my speech was muffled and indistinct.

For eight more months I was helpless. From the doctor's grave looks and my mother's obvious efforts to check her tears, I guessed that I was not expected to get better. But my mind did ceaseless battle against such a verdict. I will get better, I told myself again and again. I must dance – I must…

One evening my parents went off to the theatre leaving me in the charge of a trusted servant. All day I had been in a restless mood, impatient of inactivity, longing to get about again. How I tried, as I had done many times before, to raise myself on my pillows. I pressed my hands into the mattress and was suddenly certain that it could be done. I made another effort and found myself sitting

Nicolaeva

up. In the shock of such an achievement, I also found my voice. "I'm hungry", I said firmly, "I'd like some lamb cutlets, please".

The servant, who had been dozing beside my bed, started up in alarm.

"I'll get you some bread and milk" she said in a shaky voice. "Or an egg."

But I was tired of this sort of diet and felt that slops were no fit celebration for such a triumphant moment.

"No", I said, "I want lamb cutlets. Go on, get them quickly, or I shall die!"

Perhaps she thought this was a last request, for she threw me another frightened glance and fled away to the kitchen. When she returned with the food, I ate every scrap. Nothing had ever tasted so good! From that moment my health improved, and presently my grandmother was able to take me for a holiday in the Finnish hills. When I returned, I could think only of dancing. I was allowed to attend classes, but the doctor was cautious and ordered long periods of rest. Reading was my only compensation and I took all the books I wanted from my father's library. He never restricted my choice and I read far beyond my years; esoteric tomes, which fascinated me even though I could not always understand. Among my discoveries was the fact that dancing had long been a part of religious rituals, and I was delighted to have this justification of my own feeling.

During this period, my art teacher Sorine tried to

encourage me into another career. Years afterwards, when I met the old man at a party in Madame Pavlova's house in London he remarked rather sadly: "Ah, Mademoiselle, you are now a dancer. You could have been an artist". "Nothing you ever taught me was wasted", I assured him. "It has all helped my dancing".

As soon as I was promoted to the Senior Classes at the Imperial School, I came into much closer contact with Nicolas Legat. As a friend of my family, he had watched my progress with interest and was always ready to help me with a difficult step. Now that I was continually under his eye, he was able to give me the full benefit of his experience. My technique advanced rapidly under the constant encouragement of "Uncle Kolia" – as I had called him – and I was pleased and proud when he sometimes allowed me to watch the private lessons he gave to Anna Pavlova, Matilda Kshesinskaya, or Olga Prebrajanskaya – already famous ballerinas.

Pavlova learned a great deal from Nicolas, as she always admitted, and it is thought that it was to him she owed the extreme gracefulness of her arm movements, a special feature of the Legat teaching. He partnered her in public on many occasions, including the first time she danced the leading role in "Giselle", and in 1910, he went with her on a prolonged tour of Europe. He considered it a sad loss to Russia when she again left to make a greater name for herself in the West.

On the occasions of her return, she always asked him to dance with her, and later – when we were all in England – she came often to the Studio for Nicolas's criticism and advice. When she died, he wrote:

"I loved her as an artist, colleague and friend, and I mourn the passing of the greatest product of the greatest age of Russian art." For myself now, the goal was set. I had the finest teacher, the best examples. Dancing was to be my very life.

Nicolas Legat and Anna Pavlova

Nicolas Legat and Anna Pavlova

Nicolaeva and Nicolas Legat

CHAPTER TWO

Besides working at my dancing, I was at this time exploring further the teachings and philosophies introduced to me by my father's books. Groping for new truths, I joined the "Listeners' classes" at the University, mixing with the students and becoming involved in some of their arguments. Russia, at this time, was predominantly a military country and my sister Olga, always asserted that a man without a uniform was scarcely a man at all. I had no interest in Army types. University students were the best supporters of the Arts, and in return for their interest in ballet I was happy to let them include me in various meetings which, -- had I known it-- might have involved me in serious trouble.

Outside the tight world of the theatre and the glittering social life of the more fortunate people of Russia, there were those who had been working ceaselessly to bring about a change. Many years earlier the unrest of the middle classes had led to the foundation of a Social Democratic Party, and the workers were increasingly rebellious. Discontent was fostered and now the Liberal-Socialists were becoming stronger. Of the Bolsheviks, little had as yet been heard. I did not really understand such matters. While agreeing with my student friends that poverty and injustice ought to be wiped out, I adored the Tsar and could not see that his regime had anything to do with it. More than once he visited the Naval College and I was always thrilled to see him so close. The young recruits used to line the stairs on these occasions and when the Tsar left the building they ran after the carriage, climbing on it to wave and cheer. They were always granted a holiday in celebration. Surely, such popularity would endure.

It was about this time in my life that I was made more aware of Nicolas Legat as a person. I had the pleasant feeling that he liked me specially, yet for a long time I did not think of this as anything more than an interest in a favourite pupil whom he hoped might do him credit.

I strove hard to please my teacher and put in long hours of practice in the hope of achieving something nearer to the high standards he set. Secretly, I danced with weights on my waist and ankles, as he and Nijinsky had done, delighted when my elevation was improved by the experiment.

Then Nicolas began to show his admiration more clearly. At first, I could not believe that he could be serious, but he became more persistent,

Nicolaeva and Nicolas

following me about and telling me that he must be with me; that he could not exist without me. Only recently I had eluded another person, because I felt he encroached on my passion for dancing, but with Nicolas I knew this would be safe. Though he was so many years older, he seemed to fit into the pattern I had set for my life, and after much heart searching and some resistance, I gave in.

My family was distressed. My father reasoned with me, telling me that I could not fully realise the difficulties which would beset a young girl married to a much older man. But I had made up my mind. Nicolas was kind and gentle, with a rare fund of humour and I was content to link my life with him. We eloped, and my parents could not forgive this flouting of their wishes.

Life became rather difficult. I adored my family and hated to be cut off from them. After much discussion, Nicolas and I decided to break away temporarily from the Imperial Ballet. A European tour offered a welcome change and would take us far from family quarrels. By the time we returned, the situation might, perhaps, be eased.

Nicolas formed a small company and we achieved a two-year contract. We planned to tour France, beginning with Paris and going on to the holiday resorts.

Before we left Russia, Nicolas celebrated his twenty-five years' service at the Imperial Theatre with a special gala performance at the Maryinsky.

This evening was later described by Sir Paul Dukes

in a foreword to "Ballet Russe". Then an English tutor at the Naval College, Paul was studying music in St. Petersburg and sometimes copied manuscripts for the famous conductor Albert Coates, who allowed him the freedom of the theatre. Paul wrote:

"I shall never forget a brilliant evening at the Imperial Maryinsky Theatre in the month of January 1914. It was one of the occasions for which it was quite impossible for any but the most influential to procure tickets, but M. Teliakovsky, the Director of the theatre and a very good friend, relaxed so far as to allow me to stand just inside the door of the centre aisle. The audience was composed of the elite of the Russian nobility. The place blazed with jewels and uniforms. The strains of the National Anthem sounded, everyone rose, all eyes were fixed on the Imperial box as the Tsar, the Tsarina, and the rest of the Imperial family took their places. The orchestra, under Richard Drigo, broke into the overture and the curtain rose on the ballet "Esmeralda". It was a gala night, but it was more than that, it was a Jubilee night. One by one the chief artists emerged to meet with warm receptions – the beautiful Matilda Kshesinskaya as Esmeralda, the dignified Paul Gerdt as Frolo, the celebrated mime, Stukolkin, as Quasimodo. Then about halfway through the first act a slight figure in a green jerkin, the Poet Gringoire, was dragged on to the stage by brigands. Suddenly the performance came to a stop. The entire auditorium rose to its feet. Even the Tsar stood. On the stage, the performers deserted their positions to acclaim their colleague who remained bowing incessantly, clearly moved by this acclamation. The poet, Gringoire, was Nicolas Legat".

It was a proud moment for Nicolas. The applause lasted for more than fifteen minutes and in the last act tables were brought on to the stage and piled with gifts for him. There were telegrams too. One read: "Terpsichora Tiem bogata, Shto ti nam dala Legata". (Terpsichore has shown her riches by giving us Legat).

Yet in spite of all this adulation, Nicholas had a sense of foreboding; a feeling of impending tragedy.

"Perhaps it was a premonition", he told me afterwards. It could have been. For it transpired that this was the Tsar's last visit to the Maryinsky theatre. A few months later, the Great War broke out, followed by the still greater horrors of the revolution.

Immediately after this gala evening Nicolas and I left Russia. But the time in Paris to which we had both looked forward so eagerly was clouded with anxiety and rumours of impending war. The company had a short season at the Casino d'Enghien, but the same newspapers which reported our first performance carried also the sensational news that the journalist M. Calmette, had been assassinated by Madame Caillaux, the wife of the ex-Prime Minister. It seemed that she was incensed by a series of articles attacking her husband, which had appeared in "Le Figaro". The Minister's integrity and loyalty were in question, and there were suggestions of treasonable relationships with Germany. After the murder, M. Caillaux resigned altogether from the Government. Much later he was, indeed, tried for treason.

The affair created a great furor and the papers could speak of little else. Though the monthly magazine "Comedie Illustree" came out with a coloured cover showing Nicolas and me in a pas de deux from "Coppelia", the report, as in other papers, was cut to the minimum.

We tried to forget the threatening political scene and concentrate on our private life, and on our dancing. Nicolas renewed his acquaintance with M. Staats, now ballet-master to the company of the Grand Opera. Staats was both teacher and choreographer, while Carlotta Zambelli and M. Avelin were the principal dancers. I admired their style which was of the old French school, but I was critical of some of the classes I attended in the big room high up over the Musee, or in Staats' own classroom.

"These demoiselles seemed more concerned with their appearance than with their dancing", I told Nicolas ruefully. "Preparation for the lesson and dressing again afterwards takes up more time than the class itself. And the girls wear elegant bonnets on their heads to cover their curl-papers and make sure their hair is not disarranged!"

Had it not been for all the war talk, we could have been ideally happy. Nicolas was a charming and amusing companion. He had, of course, been to Paris several times before, and delighted in showing me the sights and introducing me to his friends.

Our performances, too, were satisfying. Nicolas, as always, danced perfectly and got many ovations; I, too, was fortunate in attracting the attention of the critics. From friends at home we heard that it was said: "A new Russian star has dawned in the Paris sky".

Before long, it became quite impossible for us to ignore politics any longer. On August 1st, Germany declared war on our beloved Russia and a few days later France and Britain were involved. Mobilisation announcements went up on Paris hoardings and members of our company began to speak as though disbandment was inevitable. Surely, there was no future for us now. In a terrible war, who would wish to watch ballet?

Presently came a welcome suggestion. Anna Pavlova wrote to Nicolas telling him that she had received an offer to take her own company to India, early in the following year. She wanted to go, but she had the usual commitment at the Palace Theatre in London. Could we take her place? Nicolas and I were delighted by the prospect. Terrible things had begun to happen in France and Paris was gloomy. On the other side of the Channel, however, it was rumoured that interest in entertainment had increased. Before the British soldiers left for the front, or when they came home on leave, everything must be as gay as possible.

We danced at the Palace Theatre in a revue called

"The Passing Show". Elsie Janis was the chief comedy star while Nicolas and I were the principal dancers. Elsie Janis was an amusing entertainer and took a variety of parts with an English, American, or Irish accent as the occasion demanded, and other artistes such a Nelson Keys supported her. At

Nicolaeva and Nicolas "The Bacchanale"

each performance, Nicolas and I danced a pas de deux of our choice, with the stage to ourselves. Though the theatre reports in the London papers were almost crowded out with war news and casualty lists, our dancing was mentioned favourably, especially when we danced in "The Bacchanale" which Pavlova had already introduced to English audiences. Some people, however, were inclined to call us "too highbrow", and this we could not understand. The Music Hall, as it existed then, was very different from what we were used to at the Maryinsky and we could only conclude that English people were not ready for this kind of art. The utmost of which they could approve was the Pas de Ruban from the ballet "La fille mal Gardee". And that only, I believe, because the weaving of the ribbons was pretty to watch. For Nicolas, with his long record of brilliant successes behind him, it was worse than for me. But he was, perhaps because he was more mature, less rebellious.

I could not help feeling hurt and disappointed, disliking, too, the petty jealousies which existed between some members of the Company. "In Russia every artiste considers himself a part of the same big family", I complained to Nicolas. "If someone is a success, others are glad for them". Nicolas would throw me one of his droll glances and say consolingly, "In every sphere there is some jealousy, I think. People are only human".

A small group of people did truly appreciate what we had to give, and we had invitations to appear on behalf of some charitable efforts and private balls. Teachers and students of serious dancing came to us also, asking for lessons, and we gave as many as we could find time for.

We acquired a willing helper, Seraphina Astafieva, who had only lately arrived from Russia. Nicolas knew her some years before in St. Petersburg where she danced in the Imperial ballet for a time. Always a little tall for a dancer, she had taken some dramatic roles, but after marrying she gave up the stage and went to live on an estate in the South of Russia – a district now menaced by the Germans. Leaving her husband, who was fighting with the White Russians, she escaped to England with no resources, and on seeing our name advertised at the Palace, came there to see us. She was really in dire straits, and glad for us to pass on to her a few of our pupils.

At the end of the Palace engagement, Nicolas and I received, among other offers, one from Sir Oswald Stoll who wanted us to appear at the London Coliseum. I remember that H. B. Irving son of the famous Henry, was appearing there in a sketch of a military character, which, it was hoped, would encour-age young men to join the Army. He was very kind to me, and so anxious that I should be happy and comfortable that he had some of the furniture from his dressing room moved into mine, which he considered more austere than it should be.

Seraphine Astafieva

Our dancing again received good notices in the press, and there were accounts of Nicholas's brilliant career. One paper commented: "If the work of his partner, Mademoiselle Nicolaeva, may be taken as a sample of his teaching, then he is truly great. Her developpes, her arabesques, are a feast for the gods. All this time Legat is 'doing nothing', just holding her, but he is doing nothing as only a master can".

Certainly, Nicolas was still my teacher. Every day then, and for many years afterwards, I had my daily lesson with him. Always I felt I could learn more, and he gladly gave me the great benefit of his vast experience. Together we worked tirelessly, our only reward the knowledge that we were a little nearer to the perfection of movement we both wished to achieve.

We toured the country with the Stoll show, but as the weeks went by homesickness became a steadily increasing distress to me. My country was at war and news of defeats or reverses were coming through to us daily. I longed to go back to Russia and see just how my parents and friends were faring. At last I could hide my anxiety from Nicolas no longer and when he challenged me with it I broke down.

"Take me home, Kolia, please", I begged. "What about our engagements", he protested. "And our pupils?" "The Management will surely release us, and Astafieva can take over the rest of our pupils".

She was delighted to do so and was proud of the testimonial with which Nicolas provided her.

There were many other Russian teachers and dancers in England. The war had led to the temporary disbandment of the Diaghilev Company, and those who could not get engagements to dance had turned to teaching as an alternative. In a current number of "The Dancing Times", this fact was commented upon, and the writer added:

"Few of ours (teachers) have passed through such severe tests. The results can surely achieve nothing but good..."

From our own point of view, there was now the question of transport. In wartime, this was a real difficulty. How should we get back to Russia?

After some delay, it was at last arranged that we should go by sea to Bergen in Norway, by minesweeper. Poor Nicolas! He had always hated travelling by sea but there was no alternative. As soon as we were on board my spirits went up, while his went down. I loved the trip, though the sea was rough and at night we were forced to travel without lights. Nicolas never once left his bunk, and for once, his sense of humour deserted him. For his sake, I wanted the voyage to end.

At Bergen, we came up against other difficulties and it sometimes seemed that we had been travelling forever. But at last, we arrived home. My mother and father, overjoyed by our safe return to them, welcomed us warmly and all former resentment was forgotten.

CHAPTER THREE

We stayed on for some while at my parents' home, for now I was to have a child. I admit to being both frightened and upset by the prospect; frightened because I was small and my hips unusually narrow, distressed because I thought this must surely be the end of my cherished hopes of stardom, the finish of my career. But I was needlessly concerned. My body was supple and athletic and responded naturally to its task, and my mother was delighted to take over my baby girl and do everything for her.

Little Anna, later called Nan by everyone, was her grandmother's joy and pride, indeed, my mother was so wrapped up in the child that there was sometimes tension between us. I was eager to get back to my dancing as soon as possible and fulfil my dream of taking all those exams I had missed earlier through ill-health, but when I could take time off from classes and practice I felt I should have the exclusive right to Nan. Once, when my mother was being possessive, we had almost a tug of war, each trying to wrest Nan from the other. Suddenly I had to laugh at the absurdity of the situation.

"Take her, Mamoushka", I said. "I can always go and do some more dancing practice".

Nicolas was highly delighted with his small daughter. He loved to indulge her every whim and would buy her anything she fancied. If at times I seemed harder, it was because I was afraid that he and my mother between them would spoil the child's character.

Nicolas had always been good with children and was able to keep them amused and happy with droll faces, funny antics, or conjuring tricks. Now I sometimes told him that he thought of Nan *and* me as his children! He had the same rallying manner for both of us, disliking to see us upset, and my diminutive size often made him want to exert his strength. I remember that once, when we were all three walking through the park together, he suddenly picked me up and set me in the pushchair with Nan on my lap, to send us coasting down a long steep slope. Passers-by showed amusement, disapproval, or consternation as Nicolas raced after us, only just managing to stop the chair at the bottom of the hill. We landed in a heap, all shrieking with laughter.

His sense of fun was always only just below the surface. When we were travelling and he wanted to keep the carriage to ourselves, he would stand at the window with a hat on each hand, trying to pretend we were full up, or he made faces to keep people out, wiggling his two false front teeth up and down with grotesque results. He told a strange story about the loss of these teeth. Years before, he was dancing with Olga Prebrajanskaya on the Maryinsky stage, spinning her strongly in a pirouette. As she came round again, she caught him sharply in the mouth with her elbow. Nicolas contrived to hide the disaster until they had taken their curtain calls. When they reached the wings, he could control himself no longer. He spat out blood and teeth, and Olga fainted!

Sometimes Nicolas's gift of mimicry was embarrassing. An unsuspecting victim with strange mannerisms would be so mercilessly reproduced that onlookers had difficulty in hiding their laughter. On many occasions, he whisked out a piece of paper and sketched a lightning caricature – or even used the cuff of his shirt! Yet he was never consciously unkind and was popular with both his friends and his public. People in St. Petersburg knew him by sight and once, when he bought a Finn's hat for a joke and insisted on wearing it, another followed suit. In no time it became the fashion, and milliners were kept busy making hats in beaver or astrakhan fur to keep pace with the demand.

A special Government mission was now being sent to Romania, not then in the war. At that time, Admiral Veselkine was controlling the Russian border, and Nicolas and I, with a small company of dancers, were sent off to join him at Reni; members of a party that would, according to custom, entertain the representatives of the two countries Russia and Romania.

With us went a balalaika orchestra under the famous conductor Boris Trejernowsky, some opera singers, musicians, and actors. On the day of our arrival, the Admiral ordered a reception and dinner party for the visitors to meet the officers of his ship, their wives, and some of the Romanian officials. It was a splendid and glittering occasion, and I was content to be a mere looker-on, but somehow the Admiral had learned who I was, and during the dinner he got up to propose a special toast. He said: "We are honoured to have with us the daughter of Admiral de Briger, the distinguished and clever man through whose hands we all passed when at the Naval College. "Officers, I ask you to salute Mademoiselle Nadia Nicolaeva and to kiss her hand". I felt embarrassed as they all paraded before me, but I was proud of this tribute to my father. The following day we were all taken across the river Danube to Bucharest. Conferences were interspersed with entertainment and the parties continued though the nights, while the flotilla lay just off the coast.

The Swan

Ballet was popular and I became a favourite. Nicolas was always glad of my successes, but many people did not know of our marriage, and he could not help showing a little jealousy when younger men paid me attention. "I always knew I was too old for you". He would say despondently. "You never seem old to me". I told him. "I could not have married someone who did not love dancing as I do". But it was, of course, pleasant to be flattered and admired. One evening when I had just finished a performance of "The Swan", a solemn announcement was made to the assembled artists and audience. King Ferdinand's aunt, the Dowager Queen of Romania (better known, perhaps, as Carmen Silva) had died. The party broke up quietly, and I found one of the Ministers at my side. "The news came earlier", he whispered in my ear. "I delayed the announcement because I wanted to see your performance. You dance beautifully, Mademoiselle".

Another night, I was seized with great pain and the Royal surgeon himself, came to examine me and diagnose a "grumbling" appendix. Because I seemed frightened, he insisted on staying beside me until I feel asleep. In the morning, he sent up to my room a beautiful arrangement of white flowers in the shape of a swan. To its neck a card was attached by a ribbon. It read: "Au cygnet qui ne meurt pas..."

Back in Petrograd, as St. Petersburg had been renamed at the outbreak of war, I began again the routine of classes and practice. I can remember sitting on a bench outside the Bolshoi theatre on the day of my exams, praying devoutly that I would be successful. I passed well, achieving the highest distinction. A credited ballerina, I was nominated a Professor to the Corps de Ballet and the Classes of Perfection.

Nicolas and I were now partners in work, as in marriage. But never could we be satisfied or smug. To an artist there is always another goal, higher than that at which he aimed before.

We had a flat in Petrograd, and another in Moscow, but for the present, it seemed better for Nan to continue living with my parents. We applied to the "English home", a club whose members were, for the most part, governesses and nannies in service with Russian families. Many of the women had returned to their own country on the outbreak of war but we were fortunate in securing the services of a Miss Ward who agreed to help look after our small daughter. Miss Ward, whom Nan called "Missy", was one of the best investments we ever made. Throughout the trials that lay ahead, she remained staunchly loyal for many years.

We had Nan with us whenever we could but ours was an irregular life, made more so by the circumstances in which the country found itself.

In Army circles, there was growing unrest and discontent. Though the soldiers had fought well it was only too clear that Russia was suffering crushing defeats, and there were heavy casualties. Officers were being nursed at Tsarskoe Selo by the Tsarina and her daughters, and other large homes took their quota. But nursing for the rank and file was poor, the men's uniforms were shoddy, and there were not nearly enough boots. Hoping to offer distraction from these hard facts the Government organised entertainment for the troops. Nicolas and I found ourselves more or less conscripted to that end and were attached to a company which would tour the various provinces throughout the south and right down to the Ukraine where the fighting was hardest. No doubt, it was intended by the Government that only our audiences should benefit, but in actual fact, we ourselves had a gay time. In every province, we were feted and feasted, each Government anxious to outdo the other in lavish hospitality. Almost every night there were supper-parties after the show, and these were lively occasions. We ballerinas, tired after our strenuous activities on stage, liked to slip off our shoes beneath the loaded tables and stretch our feet in comfort. This always caused laughter and comment for when the evening was over our escorts must dive and scramble under the tables, searching for the footwear. In the laughing confusion a victor would emerge, red-faced with several slippers for his favourite's selection. "Is this yours? No? Well, this then ..."

At the outset of the tour, some of the older ballerinas were a little aggrieved because I was included. It could be, perhaps, that they thought I had married Nicolas for the kudos his reputation would give me, though nothing could be farther from the truth. Olga Prebrajanskaya, who had, after all, known Nicolas for many years, was reported to have referred to me as "this little upstart".

For Art's sake, however, jealousy was put aside, and she came forward sometimes at rehearsal to advise me: "No, no. You must do it like this. Watch, this would be far more effective…"

The tour was so exciting and pleasant that it no doubt turned my head a little. Nicolas kept a jealous eye on my reputation however, and it was just as well, for I was young and high-spirited. Once, when an officer with whom I was dancing held me too closely for my husband's liking, he

Olga Prebrajanskaya

suddenly rushed over and pulled me away, threatening to fight my escort. "Go back to the hotel at once!" he commanded me in fury. "Why should I?" I retorted. Without answering, he picked me up in his arms and ignoring my struggles carried me out of the building and through the streets to our hotel. As he dumped me on the doorstep, I swung round and faced him. "Why do you treat me like this? Olga was dancing a fandango on the table, and you never said a word to her. You must be jealous!" But he would not confess to it. "It isn't that", he said. "But I promised your parents that I would look after you carefully". I flounced up to my room, intending not to speak to him again that night. But it was always hard to quarrel with Nicolas. He refused to take my anger seriously and made absurd grimaces and amusing remarks until at last he had me laughing.

Another time, when we were quite near the front lines an officer drove me back from a matinee performance and bragged a little. "The trenches are over there", he told me, pointing across the fields. "There's a truce on at the moment. Maybe you'd like me to show you, sometime". "Why not now?", I asked eagerly. He was alarmed. "I didn't mean it seriously", he protested.

I was determined that he should take me. I argued that if there was a truce there could be no danger, and when he would not do as I wished, I taunted him further by saying I did not suppose he had enough authority to get me through, in any case. That hurt his vanity. He parked the car and we set off across the fields. Presently we were pushing our way through the narrow trenches. No one stopped us and the ordinary soldiers, relieved temporarily of their boredom eyed me with great interest.

Suddenly the adventure took a serious turn. There was a sharp burst of gunfire and a bullet whizzed past my head. The officer threw himself upon me and forced me to lie prone. "Keep still – please! The Germans must have seen that long feather in your hat!"

With a gasp of fright, I snatched off my little green hat with its long upstanding feather and hid it under my coat. We crouched motionless for a long time, but there was no more firing. Then the officer took my hand and we crept soberly back along the trench.

As soon as we reached the car, my courage returned. "I was not really frightened", I declared. "It was exciting".

I discovered now that my escort had overstayed his time of returning to barracks and, feeling responsible, had to spend nearly an hour coaxing his superior officer to overlook it. Nicolas, who had been fuming over my long absence, was furious when I explained what had happened.

"How could you be so foolish?" he demanded. "Don't you realise? You might have been killed!"

Yet as soon as he saw that his anger had upset me, he began immediately to calm down and say that he was a silly old man and should remember that I was younger, and naturally more adventurous. He was always nagged by the difference in our ages, and now it was I who again must reassure him.

CHAPTER FOUR

When the tour of the Provinces was over, we went back to St. Petersburg. Again, the daily round of practice, classes and performances absorbed me, and I was always striving to improve my elevation or perfect a dancing step which dissatisfied me. Even Nicolas, whose life also was dedicated to the Art, would sometimes reproach me for putting so much of myself into it. "You are so absorbed in your work that you have no time, even for me", he said once. I did not take him seriously. "You should be glad, Kolia", I teased. "If I am busy there is not so much chance of my getting into mischief. Did you not hear me refuse an invitation from that nice boy who brought me flowers last evening?"

It was true that I had other and more youthful admirers. After every performance, flowers and notes were sent up to me, as they were to most of the ballerinas. But I rarely went to a party which did not include Nicolas. In any case, I knew that late nights were bad for my dancing.

Though I liked to get to bed as early as possible, I often read far into the night, for it was almost my only chance to pursue my interest in the philosophers and thinkers of every age. It was an interest that Nicolas could not share. He had always a curiously uncomplicated attitude to life; it was part of a childlike quality that made him particularly lovable.

Though some members of the ballet company had a gay time off-duty, the official Russian attitude to Art itself was austere, as it had always been. At the Maryinsky and Bolshoi theatres dancers were not allowed to wear even the simplest jewelry, unless it was in keeping with the role. I remember that once I forgot to remove a small string of pearls. Almost as soon as I left my dressing room the stage manager noticed them. "Take that necklace off, please, Nicolaeva", he said. "It will distract the attention of the audience".

It was different in France, I reflected a trifle rebelliously as I obeyed. There many of the dancers wore glittering necklaces given to them by special patrons. It was whispered that patronage was used to promote a dancer from the back rows of the stage to the front.

"Perhaps it is better this way", I admitted to Nicolas afterwards. "In Russia we know that recognition comes only with hard work and perseverance, which reminds me, Kolia, that it is time I had my lesson with you…"

Now into our private world and even into the self-contained world of the theatre, anxiety began to penetrate. The war was proving disastrous for Russia, and American intervention had come too late. Many soldiers deserted from the front, and in the cities mounted police patrolled continuously. Some shops put up their shutters and food was becoming scarce.

By the beginning of 1917, the clouds that had been massing on the political horizon looked even more threatening; the workers were in a stage of rebellion. Though some concessions had been made by the Government they were not considered adequate. Behind the people were piled the grievances of centuries and the disorganisation caused by the war and its problems created circumstances favourable to a stand.

In March, the Tsar was forced to abdicate. He was banished to Ekaterinburg in the Ural Mountains where he and his family remained under close arrest. Nicolas, like many another staunch monarchist, grieved when he heard the news.

At my parents' home, we had many an anxious discussion. The former Director of the Naval College having been arrested on suspicion some time before, my father had taken his place. He was beloved by all his pupils and was working desperately hard to keep the college going. Only by tenacity and single-minded concentration on the job in hand could he help the students to finish their training in these difficult times. How long would he be able to carry on, we wondered. In spite of his selflessness, or even because of it, was he likely to become a marked man if real trouble should come?

We talked round and round the subject – the whole family in conclave together – but my father was certain he must go on. Nicolas was optimistic, as always. Perhaps, he argued, some of the ugly rumours were exaggerated. Perhaps the trouble would blow over as it had done before. "I hope you are right", I said soberly, and held Nan closer each time we said goodbye.

The new and hastily formed Government of Liberals under Kerensky now urged the Army and the people to stand steadfastly together. Kerensky, however, wanted to continue the war, where the ordinary Russian citizen was sick to death of a conflict that had brought to him nothing but disaster and privation. One could scarcely blame them, yet it was obvious that someone must offer a solution.

Peace at any price was the declared aim of the extreme Radicals – the Bolsheviks – and many were now prepared to support them. Parties of workers and deserters began to take the law into their own hands. They broke into houses, ostensibly to search for arms and find out who was against them. Then, inflated with unaccustomed power, they threw furniture about and left everything in disorder, sometimes dragging their enemies into the streets and dispensing summary justice.

The daily ration of bread had fallen from one pound a day to only half a pound; then to a quarter. Soon, it was feared, there might be none at all. Men, women and children raided the shops in desperation and overthrew barricades. Horses lay dying in the streets because there was no grain to spare for them.

Food had never bothered me greatly, but I marveled at Nicolas's continued cheerfulness under these conditions. He had an enormous appetite and once caused quite a sensation in Budapest by eating at one meal fourteen eggs, a large beefsteak, and a pudding; the whole washed down by several glasses of beer! With his spare frame, one wondered where he could put it all, but no doubt, his immense energy quickly burned it up.

In spite of the troubled times, life in the theatre went on in much the same way as usual. Ballet and Opera were an accepted part of the Russian scene and audiences as large and enthusiastic as ever.

In the autumn of this year, Chaliapin was guest artist at the People's Theatre, Narodny Dom, singing in a season of opera for which Nicolas arranged the ballets, while I danced in them.

Chaliapin was then about forty-four, at the very height of his fame. A shoemaker's apprentice in his boyhood, he progressed via a minor opera company to the Maryinsky itself, though it was not until after he left there that he became well known outside Russia.

He was in Europe when the war broke out, but he insisted on returning to Russia where he established two small hospitals at his own expense. Acclaimed by everyone, popularity had not spoiled him.

At the theatre one evening, I danced Venus in the ballet in which Faust is tempted with all the delights Mephistopheles can offer, and in this scene the singing is less import than the dancing. I had just arrived back in my dressing room when there was a great hammering at my door, and I heard Chaliapin calling me.

"Nicolaeva, come quickly! They are asking for you".

When I opened my door a crack and stared at him, he repeated: "Come along. They want you!" "No, no", I protested. "It is you they're applauding. It must be…"

He did not wait for further arguments. Stepping forward, he swept me into his huge embrace and carried me along the corridor and back to the wings. People in the audience were still shouting and clapping, for Chaliapin always kept them waiting between curtain calls — he said it made them appreciate him more. When they saw him return to the stage with my small white-clad figure in his arms, they surged forward, roaring their enthusiasm. Chaliapin held me tightly so that I could not escape and bowed and bowed again. To him such an occasion probably meant little, but for me it was an unforgettable moment; allowed by his generosity.

We were still at the Narodny Dom when St. Petersburg was beset by rumours that the Bolsheviks were about to seize the railway stations, the Bank, and the power stations. That evening the company assembled as usual however. Only Chaliapin failed to arrive.

We stood about in groups, talking gravely about the news and wondering what could have happened to the great singer. The Stage Manager paced up and down in agitation and went once more to delay the ringing up of the curtain. A few minutes later, he was called to the telephone and we gathered round, hoping to learn something.

"Yes – yes", we heard the Stage Manager say. "What is it? Where are you?" The expression on his face became more and more concerned. At last he rang off and with a gesture of despair, turned to face us. "He says he cannot get through. The streets are jammed tightly with crowds and the Nikolaevsky Bridge has been raised!"

There were murmurs of horror and concern. I caught my breath and turned to Nicolas in fear. On the farther side of the bridge was the Naval College. My parents were there, and with them was little Nan!

"Kolia, what will happen? Will they be all right, do you think?"

I knew that my husband must share my anxiety, though he patted my shoulder and tried to speak calmly.

"They will be all right. You must not worry". "How can I help it?", I replied.

I clung to his hand for comfort, my imagination picturing the dramatic scenes which might very well be taking place. All around us were other members of the company, many of them afraid for those they loved.

What of our own safety? What lay in store for all of us? For Russia?

But already the Director had instructed Chaliapin's understudy to be ready to go on stage immediately. The orchestra began the overture. For the moment our fears must be put aside. In the old tradition of the theatre, the show must go on. Anything else was impossible.

Throughout the rest of the evening, I moved in a

kind of trance, my feet and my body obeying the commands I gave them, but with none of the usual joy. The whole company responded well and few, if any, in the audience could have guessed at the fears and anxiety which lay behind our performances. No doubt, those who watched us had their own misgivings. We were at least allowing them a brief respite.

As soon as the curtain came down for the last time, I queued for the telephone and tried to get through to my home. When at last I took my turn, the wires were jammed with other enquiries, and for some time I heard nothing but a jumble of broken conversations. Then at last came my mother's voice.

"Are you all right?" I asked. "Is everyone safe?" "Of course, child, of course". My mother's tone sounded strange and I thought she was hiding something from me. Before I could question her further she went on hurriedly, "Do not attempt to come here, Nadia. The bridge is raised, and we are surrounded by the Red Army. Your father is talking to an officer now".

"What is he saying? What do they want to do?" I cried. But already there was a click at the other end of the line, and we were cut off. I clung to Nicolas, trembling. "Something awful is happening there. I know it".

"Come", said Nicolas gently, leading me away. "There is nothing we can do now. We'll go to my sister's home for the night. Tomorrow we may be able to find out more". As always when I was upset, he tried to cheer me by jokes and quaint expressions. But this time I could not appreciate them. I was sick with apprehension.

Outside the theatre, the streets were jammed with milling crowds. People were arguing, fighting, or merely standing around in groups to see what would happen. Farther down the street was Madame Kshesinskaya's great house. She was in Europe and the place had been taken over by the Central Committee. Speakers stood on the balcony shouting, and demanding support for the rebellion. Cheers and booing almost drowned their words. Everyone seemed excited.

I shrank against my husband as he pushed a way for me through the crowd. Some recognised us but none tried to molest us. Throughout all the troubled times which followed I never knew of any dancer in real danger. Both sides recognised us as artists and regarded us as beings apart from politics; as indeed we were.

When at last we arrived at my sister-in-law's house, I tried to take heart from the encouraging words with which they hoped to cheer me. Now, however, it was I who had a premonition of disaster. It proved to be the disaster of separation. Six long years were to elapse before I saw my parents and my child again.

CHAPTER FIVE

Now days and nights were full of terror. Hundreds of arrests were made, and there was the continual sound of shooting and fighting; the shocking sight of brutality and sudden death. Throughout our own difficulties I suffered acute anxiety about Nan and my parents from whom I had received no word since my agitated telephone call. Rumours came through that the Naval College was guarded and surrounded. I did not know whether my family was still besieged, or if they had escaped. I tried hard not to give way to fears that the worst might have befallen them, but in moments of depression, I owned to myself that this was indeed possible.

People one had taken for granted now came out in new colours and allegiance hitherto hidden was flaunted. I discovered with surprise that Rose my dresser and manicurist, was an influential member of the Bolshevik party. Rose was a big, good natured woman who had seemed far too easy-going for politics. I found it difficult to adjust my ideas and concede the respect due to her position.

She could, however, be useful to me, so I hid my surprise and threw myself upon her mercy. "The Nikolaevsky Bridge is still guarded, and I must find out something about my family", I said. "Will you try to get me a pass?"

Rose refused at first. But she had always been devoted to me, and when I persisted, day after day, she agreed at last to see what she could do. "But if I get the pass it will not be for you, Madame", she finished emphatically. "Your place is at the theatre, and you might get hurt. Someone else must go".

I did what I could to persuade her against this decision, but she was adamant. Unless I promised not to use the pass myself, she would do nothing about obtaining it. My sister, Olga, pointed out that it was better that she should go, in any case, for she was married to a wealthy Guards officer with an estate in Kiev and her own position was open to question. If she could reach the family, she might be able to arrange not only their escape, but her own. In the south, tempers were quieter, and the food situation not so desperate.

Olga

Rose managed to get the pass and Olga and I bid each other an affectionate and dramatic farewell. Afterwards I suffered anxiety and some remorse, wondering if I should have allowed her to go on such a dangerous mission. "If only Rose had let *me* go!" I said. Nicolas made a comical grimace and glanced at me; his blue eyes quizzical. "But you do not wish to escape to Kiev, I think, as Olga does?"

I had to admit that he was right. The political implications of the struggle meant little to me. Some months before, I had listened to a long and impassioned speech by Lenin and had been unable to come down on one side or the other. Tyranny over the workers was hateful, I agreed, yet was this new tyranny a real improvement? I only knew that while those responsible for the present regime in Petrograd were willing for theatre and ballet performances to continue, I wanted to take part in them. Nicolas felt he same. We could not imagine another life or contemplate an existence without the dancing we loved so much.

It was some time before news of my family filtered back to us; longer still before letters confirmed our hopes. With my other sister, Xenia, who had lost her husband in the fighting and was left a widow with a small boy, they were now all in Kiev where, for the present at least, life was more or less normal. Olga reported that my mother and father had been through some dreadful experiences. Soldiers had swarmed into their apartments in the Naval College, searching drawers and cupboards for incriminating documents and taking away some possessions. After which they had been virtually prisoners until Olga and Vladimir had engineered an escape.

Relieved of some of my anxiety I felt able to cope with the situation in which Nicolas and I found ourselves. The new regime had, of course, caused a serious break in the traditions of the Maryinsky; the Im-

perial Arms and the eagles were removed immediately
and the attendants at
the theatre no longer
wore livery. There was a
very different type of
audience too; lor-
ry-loads of facto-
ry-workers were depos-
ited in the foyer each
evening and former po-
litical refugees sprawled
in the Tsar's box. Nico-
las, though he kept
cheerful as always, de-
plored the degradation

Xenia and son Nicki

of the Maryinsky which had been the scene of so
many grand occasions.

"When I look round at this drab audience, I cannot
help remembering", he said.

However, we were thankful that we still had an audience, an appreciative one to whom we made no concessions. The standard of performances was a high as
ever.

Certainly, these were dramatic times to be living in,
and we felt ourselves to be walking on the knife-edge
of danger. Yet we lived no hole-and-corner existence
but moved about freely, going to and fro to the theatre
without trouble, or joining the crowds to witness some
event of special significance. I was with Nicolas and

his nephew, Anatole Oboukhoff, outside the prison when the doors were opened, and the political prisoners set free. People cheered the unshaven, wild-looking men who surged into the streets, but I shrank back, somewhat horrified by the knowledge that these rebels would now be given positions of authority. Nicolas made a joke of it all, saying:

"Fine – fine. Let us clap and cheer. But where is the music? Even for so unusual a ballet one must surely have orchestral accompaniment!"

We were both deeply grieved when we heard, later, that the Tsar and his family had been wiped out of life in a few horrifying moments. I remembered the cheering students; the smiling and waving that had formerly accompanied all the Tsar's movements. How quickly the tide of popularity could turn!

The tide had turned, too for Chaliapin. At first, he was well treated by the new Government; given many privileges and made a member of a Committee set up for preserving works of Art. Although he had previously had great sympathy for the workers he could not hide his disapproval of the way in which mob rule had so quickly replaced the old order. This was resented and he became suspected of subversive activities. His flat was ransacked, his money and goods confiscated. We heard later that he and his family were near to starvation; then that he had fled.

These things troubled me. Before the revolution, life had been peaceful and pleasant for only the more fortunate, and my intelligence told me that there was justice in the new claims. But the way of staking these claims was surely unnecessarily harsh.

We dancers, however, were not molested – even when things were at their worst. We were encouraged to form our own committee of management and were subject only to the very highest authority. If at times the soldiers tore the theatre scenery to pieces and pulled down the heavy curtains, they did so only perhaps to make wrappings for their bootless feet. For poverty and hardship ran hand in hand with this so-called glorious revolution.

There was scarcely any fuel to be had and as more people flocked into the city, accommodation was at a premium. Several people had to share one room, with little or no privacy, and all were reduced to the drab-best and shabbiest of clothes.

At first artists' flats were protected by law, and Nicolas and I still had our home. We used only one room, however, for the weather was bitterly cold and we had to conserve our small stock of fuel.

In spite of difficulties, we did our best to maintain some of the standards of our previous life. Nicolas had always been inordinately proud of his beautiful hands and long slender feet. In more gracious days, he kept in his room shelves full of shoes the same colour as his suits, or to match a favourite tie; he was forever filing and polishing his fingernails. Now he shined with loving care what was left of his stock of shoes or crouched over the meagre warmth of the stove to manicure his hands as scrupulously as ever. One of *my* greatest pleasures was my daily bath; so now, even in the coldest weather, I set a small zinc bath on top of the fire until the water was lukewarm, then lowered it to the floor so that I could splash myself all over.

In those days a few wood blocks or a basket of stout twigs were infinitely more precious gifts than all the flowers and chocolates I had received in the old days, and nothing gave me greater pleasure than a fresh cake of scented soap! Nicolas laughed at the bargains I made. I have danced for only the reward of a pound of butter, and once in a factory where my pay was to be wood for the fire. After my performance, I was presented with two stout tree trunks which Nicolas and a couple of boys from the theatre dragged home through the streets on a sledge. I can see my husband now – joking as usual – bowing left and right in mockery and declaiming cheerfully to anyone who would listen: "Behold Nicolas Legat – first soloist to the Tsar – now at your service for the hauling of wood!"

Attendance at the theatre was subject to the strictest discipline. Excuses for absence were frowned upon, and only one concession was made. If the temperature went below zero, we need not dance. We carried a thermometer about with us to prove it, but it often *felt* like zero when it was not!

Endurance was a necessity. Someone, at this time, introduced me to cocaine, saying it would give me the ability to keep going. I have always gloried in experiment and I could see no reason why I should not try it. I took it for a whole month before I realised that it was spoiling my dancing, and that the pleasant feeling of relaxation must be paid for by a slackening of standards. I remember walking down the Nevsky Prospect, standing on the bridge and trying to find the courage to throw the bottle into the water. I thought to myself – why throw it away? I could probably sell it for money. Then again, I must not help others downhill. In desperation, I took some more cocaine to help the decision, then flung the bottle into the Neva and turned away. Now the street seemed to float before my eyes; first uphill, then down. Stumbling along, I ran into Walensky, the critic, a small ugly man with a long nose. I flung myself into his arms, kissing him in the relief of seeing a familiar face. Later he came round to our flat, enquiring from Nicolas.

"Is Nadia all right? She was so strange this afternoon".

It was certainly a hard life though not without compensation. Nicolas and I still had our work, our daily lesson together, and the privilege of dancing in the big familiar theatre to the well-loved music. At such times we could imagine it all as before and close our minds to the continued bitterness, to the fighting and arrests. In our more optimistic moments, we even persuaded ourselves that everything would settle down; that life would eventually become as it was in the old days.

But in the December of that year Lenin made a proclamation declaring all private property to be now under the ownership of the State; all bank accounts would be closed. I knew that our own most treasured possessions, and those of my parents', would be confiscated. It was hard to bear.

Even the theatre was now tainted with prejudice. No foreign items must be included in the programmes – even the well-known "Pas de Ruban" was banned. Being of French origin it was argued by ignorant authority that it could not be other than indecent.

The new Directorate of the theatre also had the power to make arbitrary decisions regarding the dancers, and suddenly Nicolas and I were told that we were to be transferred from the Maryinsky to the Bolshoi, in Moscow.

"Why?" I asked Nicolas, apprehensive. "Is it, do you think, because you once danced for the Tsar?"

He smiled and shook his head. "I shouldn't think so. After all, the two theatres have always been interchangeable, and now that the Government is making Moscow its headquarters, the Bolshoi may even take precedence".

Certainly, the two theatres had always been closely linked; but there was a subtle difference in the audiences, and performances were angled with that in mind. Petrograd was cosmopolitan; here lived the cream of society. In Moscow rich industrialists predominated. In these days of levelling and equality however, there would, perhaps, be little difference.

For one reason at least, I welcomed the move south. We should be nearer the family and might have news of them. It was so long since we had heard, and the silence had begun to weigh upon me.

I little knew that my family had already left Russia. Because of the chronological order, I must relate events of which I only heard details later.

The sanctuary my parents and sisters had hoped to find in Kiev soon became untenable, for now the workers were inflamed against anyone with wealth, and especially those who had been in the employ of the Tsar. Many of Olga's servants remained loyal and would have done anything to save her home from molestation, but outside influences were too strong, and they could only give a warning when attack was imminent. This they did, and now joined by my brother-in-law the family fled southwards again to Odessa, where another relative lived.

Again, the villagers were loyal at first, but the poison of the revolutionaries was spreading, and one night a mob of rough men came hammering at the door of the house, threatening to break it down.

My mother had established firmly in her mind that Lenin was Anti-Christ, or "the devil". She made a quick prayer before the silver icon of which I spoke earlier, then rising from her knees and taking the icon with her went calmly to the front door and opened it. As she held up the sacred image before the crowd, the men backed away, murmuring; then ran off down the drive as if the very 'devil' himself was after them!

Unfortunately, this miracle had no lasting effect. On the outskirts of Odessa, the French were attacking, and the Communists were out for revenge on those who had, in their opinion, been a party to such a situation. They came to the house again and arrested my father and Olga's husband, saying they were to be shot. Mother and Olga were distressed and terrified. In a desperate bid to save the men they loved, they managed to smuggle a message to the French authorities, begging them to act quickly on their behalf. The French Commandant came to their rescue and made a bargain with the rebels; the lives of my father and brother-in-law in return for twenty Communist prisoners. The offer was accepted, the two men were released and the whole family joined other refugees under the protection of the French who were organising boats which would carry them across the Black Sea to safety. My father was put in command of a ship which should have accommodated two hundred; instead, five hundred people were crowded on board.

By the time this ship reached Constantinople where it should have landed its passengers, they were almost starving, and one had developed a mild case of smallpox. The quarantine flag had to be run up and the refugees were forbidden entry. Conditions became almost intolerable and my father sent out distress signals which were ignored by all but a small English frigate which came alongside to offer help. The Captain took off the man with smallpox and sent him to hospital, at the same time cabling England for further instructions. By gracious permission of His Majesty, King George V, a message came back offering the refugees hospitality in Malta. Xenia and her small son, Nicki, were allowed to travel on to Germany where Vladimir was, and Miss Ward, being a British subject, had no difficulty in getting back to England. The rest of the de Briger family stayed in Malta for a year, during which time my young daughter, Nan, mixed with all and sundry in the camp and knew a life that would have horrified me, had I known of it. But I did not know…

When the camp in Malta was broken up, my family was given travelling facilities and went to Italy. Here, Olga and her husband remained for some time; while my parents and Nan went on to join Vladimir in Germany. He, however, had his own family to support, besides my sister, Xenia. His resources were taxed to the uttermost, and things went from bad to worse.

Mother and Father with Nan in Malta

My father, however, was a Director of the Anglo-Baltic Shipping Company, and when he heard that the London office was still functioning and would give him a post there, he left for England. Mother and Xenia, with the two children, were admitted at last to a camp for displaced persons and again Nan was subjected to appalling conditions – she told me afterwards that she and her cousin used to search the ground in the beer gardens, after a Saturday night, in the hope of finding a few coins....

Fortunately, my father was presently able to send money for them to join him, which they did. Later Olga and her husband also came to England and found a house in Golders Green where they could all be together. Though they had every reason to believe that Nicolas and I had died in the early days of the revolution, a faint hope still lingered.

When Paul Dukes returned to London to be knighted for his services to the Foreign Office in reporting on the present regime in Russia, he and my father met by chance. Paul reported seeing us in Petrograd and thought it likely we were still there.

The family, of course, was overjoyed. On hearing that the first Trade Commission was shortly to be sent to Russia, my father entrusted one of its members with a letter which eventually reached us. But when Nicolas and I went to Moscow, we knew nothing of this.

CHAPTER SIX

Three hundred miles separate Petrograd from Moscow, but the contrast is more marked than this distance would suggest. Petrograd was – still is I suppose – somewhat Western in style, while Moscow with its heavy architecture, its curious domes and spires, is linked in appearance with the East.

When Nicolas and I arrived there, it was to find that our own flat had been commandeered. We were given another in a block quite close to the theatre, but it was difficult to feel grateful for day or night the shooting was apt to break out with no warning.

The flat dwellers made a rota of defence, detailing two of their number to remain always on guard against fires or looting. One day it was Nicolas's turn for duty, and I had started out for rehearsal when a burst of gunfire sent me scuttling into the nearest doorway.

By the clever ruse of going in first as tourists and taking over at a given signal, the rebel forces had earlier commandeered all the biggest hotels. But the Monarchists were still holding on to some Government properties from which they could not be dislodged.

Now, in the lull between firing, I hurried along the street, keeping close to the walls. On one side of the building which had once been the Imperial School was the Hotel Metropole, under Bolshevik command; on the other side the Post Office and the railway station. Seizing my opportunity, I dashed across the street and into the School, only to find that no one else from the

Company had arrived. Obstinately determined to justify my presence, I decided to rehearse on my own, but as I pirouetted across the floor of the great rehearsal room, the firing broke out again and a bullet pierced the window and flew past my head. When another followed it, and yet another, I decided that obstinacy could be taken too far. Nicolas would be worrying. I had better go back home.

On the way there, a drunken man followed me. I was terrified but as he lurched closer, evil-smelling and unkempt, indignation gave me courage. I dealt him a sharp sideways kick that sent him sprawling into the gutter.

"I'm sure that must be the first time a battement frappé has been used with quite the same effect", I told Nicolas on my return, trying to make light of the incident for his sake. "It is a good thing I have such strong legs!"

Life in Moscow was uncomfortable; terrifying at times. It seemed strange that people could still be willing to attend ballet performances. The food situation was even worse than it had been in Petrograd, and Nicolas declared that he longed for a good square meal. When at last a new proposition was put to us, it seemed that any change must be better than none.

The new Government was serious in its intention to widen the outlook of the workers. Artists of all kinds were being pressed to join companies that would tour the country, and we saw the scheme through the rose-coloured glasses of an agent's propaganda. We were told that special railway carriages would be fitted up with beds and living quarters; costumes and décor would be lent by the Maryinsky theatre; food would be good and plentiful.

It was not until we had agreed to go on one of these Government "Light and Culture" tours that we began to see what it might entail. Then my relief at leaving Moscow changed to dismay.

"There will be no theatres in these far-distant villages", I told Nicolas. "And peasants cannot be expected to understand our kind of dancing".

Nicolas had the happy quality of acceptance.

"We are surely not so difficult to understand", he said. "All kinds of people have watched our performances and enjoyed them. In any case, we are not allowed to refuse, and it is too late now for escape".

"But I've heard that agitators will be travelling with the Company", I argued. "Artists should not get mixed up in politics". "They cannot make dancing politics", Nicolas pointed out gently. "We are asked only to dance".

Always I must be seeking reasons, for small issues as well as the larger one of our very existence. Now I told myself that I must prove some of the philosophies I had studied and resign myself to discipline. What Nicolas said was true. We had been asked only to dance. That is what we both wanted to do, and we must do it as and where we could.

It was just as well we did not know exactly what we were in for. Conditions on this tour were appalling. The weather was bitterly cold and our little company of six dancers, a pianist, a cellist and a singer were herded together uncomfortably in old railway carriages which were hooked on to trains and moved from place to place as authority directed.

We performed in village halls and factories with no scenery. Stages were often mounted on the night of our arrival; too high, or with boards that creaked and rocked with every step. There were two Administrators in charge, one a political speaker, the other directing the artistic side. Both were staunch supporters of the new regime, but kindly disposed towards us.

"At least you were right about appreciative audiences", I told Nicolas, peeping between the thin stage curtains at the simple peasants who sat in rows on the floor, wearing fur hats and thick scarves, and smoking and spitting. "They may be ignorant, but they seem to like our dancing".

After each performance, an Administrator would come on stage and harangue the audience. "We have brought you pearls from the Tsar's own crown", he boomed lustily. "Once the ballet was only for Emperors and Kings. Now - under our new and splendid Government – it is for you". But already the audience, realising there was an end of the dancing they had come to see, was filing out through the doors. They were no more interested in politics than we were.

It became obvious to those in charge that their tactics must be changed. Now those who wanted to see the ballet must sit through a long political talk first. This they did, hiding their unwillingness with inscrutable expressions and puffing on their pipes until one could scarcely see across the hall. One of the Administrators nicknamed me "Bitaia Carta", meaning 'trump card'. "You bring in my best audience", he said with a huge laugh. I do not think the lectures really penetrated these untutored minds. The people clapped and cheered the new Government dutifully when it seemed expected of them, but one day I heard some of them shouting: "Long live the Tsar and his new Queen 'Revolution'…"!

Remuneration for our dancing was — to our horror- given in goods, not money, for the villagers were very poor and the expedition must pay its way. Before each performance a large empty sack was placed by the door. As the people filed past they dropped into the sack any contribution they could make; rice, semolina, sugar and salt all mixed up together with a few potatoes and other root vegetables. When we complained we were told with a shrug: "It cannot be helped. You must sift it". Sometimes the carriages in which the company travelled were moved into a siding while more important traffic was taken through. Daily practice was an essential for me, though for this I must perhaps cross frozen ground to some abandoned goods van. I have even practised on a deserted part of the railway station itself! Nicolas came with me of course, playing on his violin and correcting my faults with the same serious dedication as when he stood before me in the class-room at the Imperial School. He never complained, though often it was so cold that his fingers could scarcely hold the bow. To both of us this daily ritual was so absorbing that we could almost forget the snow drifting through the cracks in the roof on to our hair, and the icy winds that whirled around our bodies.

The guards of the train sometimes came to watch, their glances friendly. Even if they could not under-stand our enthusiasm, I think they gave it a grudging admiration; this they expressed in all sorts of strange ways, such as keeping our part of the carriage a little cleaner than others, bringing us extra food, or teaching me how to make their favourite beetroot borscht, which was always served with sour cream.

To our audiences no doubt we seemed glamorous indeed. They were too ignorant to realise that we were totally unused to the hardships of such a life, and though the glories of our costumes were fading fast with constant packing and unpacking, they meant colour and beauty to those who had never before glimpsed such things. At each stop, we gained new admirers who crowded round us after the performance and gazed at us with something like awe. It was a constant wonder to them that I danced on my toes; one man wanted to know if my feet had been cut across; another thought I might have springs fixed to my shoes. I was always quite willing to prove to them that I had normal feet, and that my only aid was the blocking in the toes of my ballet shoes.

The tour, originally planned for three months, dragged on and on. In vain, we remonstrated with the Administrator, pointing out that the time for returning to Moscow was well overdue, that now even our papers were not valid. But our expedition, I think, must have rewarded those in charge better than it did us, and they wanted to continue. One of the men did consent at last to return to Moscow and take out new papers for us, and Nicolas – at the last moment – insisted on going too. He hoped to persuade the authorities to refuse an extension, but in any case, he would be able to get one or two things we needed from the flat.

I never knew what influence Nicolas used with the Administrator to persuade him to take him on the journey, but it was not sufficient to terminate the tour. When the papers came back they were all in order, and we must go on. Nicolas told amusing tales of his journey to Moscow. Trains were constantly inspected by police and at every stop he had to slip in with the prisoners under arrest. They, of course, were not asked to produce papers!

One day, when we were dancing at a village far south, a girl called Parashka came to me after the performance and told me a pitiful tale about her unkind husband.

"Your dancing is so beautiful, Madame, that I am sure you have a good heart", she gulped. "Take me with you when you leave. I beg you. I will be your maid and will work for nothing". I was touched by the girl's evident misery. Talking it over with Nicolas, we agreed to help her. "Come along when it is dark, and we'll try to smuggle you in", I told Parashka. "Then, when we are at a safe distance, I might persuade the Commissars to let you stay".

When we arrived back after the performance that evening, however, it was to find that the railway carriages had been moved from the station and into a siding some distance away. "Poor Parashka!" I whispered to Nicolas. "She will never find us here".

Much later that night the carriage was shunted back into the station. I glanced out of the window and, to my surprise, saw Parashka dancing on the platform, and surrounded by railway workers and guards who were clapping and shouting. She broke off when she saw me and ran across, almost incoherent with relief.

It seemed that the guards had found her wandering on the line and had arrested her. Because of her agitation, and the different patois of the country village, they had misunderstood her explanation. "If you are one of the dancers, then you must prove it", they told her, and she had done her best.

Good humoured after their entertainment, the guards made no objection to Parashka joining up with us. There was no doubt that she made herself useful, but unfortunately, she had little control where men were concerned, and was always going off with one or another of them. Presently I noticed that her figure was changing, but when I mentioned it to her, she gazed back at me with an innocent expression. "Yes, indeed Madame. It is something inside which is blowing me up like this", she agreed. Very soon, it was apparent just what that something was, and we had to leave Parashka at the nearest hospital to have her baby.

The tour seemed interminable. We travelled on and on, right across to the Caspian Sea, then up to Siberia. We could not complain of hunger, but cold and exhaustion must be faced all the time. Often we made our change of costume in the carriages and then walked three miles or more to the hall where we were to dance. One of the Administrators seemed always to be a little on my side, and sometimes he would procure a sledge, and pull me along on it.

We had no money, so there was no possibility of escaping to better conditions. Presently the constant travelling and hardship began to undermine my health, and one night I felt so ill that Nicolas went off to tell the Administrators it would be impossible for me to dance.

"I must try to find a doctor", he said.

In every town now, of course, there were new Administrators, some were good, some bad. In this village, those in charge were arrogant; puffed up with the new power for which they were not fitted. Unknown to Nicolas, they would not accept the excuses made on my behalf and insisted on sending their own emissary to see if I was shamming.

As I lay on my rough bed, feeling very ill, the door of the carriage was thrown open.

"I am a doctor", said the man who stood there. He crossed to my side, felt my pulse, and made me put out my tongue. Then he thrust a glass into my hand. "Of course, you must dance. Get up. You will feel fine when you drink this wine".

I could only stare at him helplessly. I had not the strength to sit up, let alone put on my clothes. Then he threatened me, saying that if I did not get up he would have to give me a complete examination. At that moment, Nicolas appeared in the doorway. The real doctor pushed the bogus one aside and bent over me, announcing gravely: "This woman has a very high temperature. It is pneumonia, I should think. I forbid her to move".

Even the genuine doctor was of little use, for he knew only three remedies; bicarbonate of soda, castor oil, or leeches. These last he now attached behind my ears, and I felt too weak even to voice my horror.

Nicolas nursed me through my illness, but I never fully recovered my strength and remained pale and thin.

"I shall write to the Government at Moscow", Nicolas said worriedly. "You cannot go on without a holiday".

His pleas were answered at long last. We went to the Caucasus at the Government's expense, but it was not the sort of holiday for a person in my frail condition.

The Caucasians were wild people and the disordered state of the country enabled them to make constant raids on the villages, looting and plundering at will. In the place where we were staying, there was a nightly curfew and doors and windows were barred against possible intruders. In spite of this, the sound of shots and curses ran through the nights, disturbing my sleep. I lay in terror, expecting the marauders to break into the house and carry me off.

There was no excitement now about walking the knife-edge of danger. Only my deep inner conviction that the mind rules the body saved me from utter despair.

At the end of our holiday, we were sent back to Moscow. Nicolas hid his concern from me, but I knew

later that he had determined to get me out of Russia
if it was possible.

CHAPTER SEVEN

It was when we returned to Moscow that my father's letter was at last delivered to me. Nicolas and I read the closely written pages together many times, exulting in the news that the family was safe, even though hundreds of miles away. There must still be some sadness in the thought that Nan was growing up without us. How long would it be before we should all meet again?

In Moscow, it seemed that everything was changed. There was no firing now, and the State School of the Bolshoi theatre was attended by about two hundred day-pupils, handpicked from the masses. Nicolas again became ballet-master and we danced the principal parts in many stage productions.

Every now and then he would ask me how I was feeling. "Much better", I always assured him, and when he remarked that I certainly did not look it I was disturbed, for secretly, I knew that I had not the same stamina as before.

No one seemed aware of any deficiency, however, and I was much in demand. Nicolas ceased to comment, and it was not until much later that I knew his intention to get me away from Russia was never abandoned.

I was dancing in the ballet "The Hump-backed Horse" one evening. My partner – a young man called Victor Smoltzoff, who had not long graduated from the State School – hurried over to me as I stood in the wings, awaiting my entrance cue. His eyes shone with excitement.

"Nadia, I have to tell you-- we're leaving Russia", he whispered. I turned towards him startled, then decided he must be joking. "Hush", I said. "We're on in a moment". "I mean it, Nadia. Uncle Kolia is packing now, and we are all three of us leaving tonight".

"Uncle Kolia" was the name by which Nicolas was known to most of the young dancers. But already the music was beginning, and there was no time to question Smoltzoff further or argue. As always, I wished to lose myself in the character I portrayed. I was determined Smoltzoff should not distract me.

My partner, however, was determined to make me aware of him. As we danced, he continued to give me meaningful glances and at one point managed to mutter: "You must take all your things home with you tonight. You won't be coming back. We shall be free!"

Was he mad? I asked myself. Could there be any truth in what he said? But surely, if Nicolas were planning something, he would have told me.

As soon as our dance was over, I turned to Smoltzoff. "What is the matter with you tonight? Are you making fun of me?"

"No, it's true, Nadia", he insisted in a low voice. "We're leaving Russia. Listen carefully, Uncle Kolia has sent you a message. Tonight, you must sign off rehearsals for three days – you know we're allowed three a month – and take all your things with you. I have a

doctor's certificate saying my knee needs rest and Kolia is planning the new ballet. We'll be on our way to
the border before they miss us".

"But why, if it is true, – are *you* telling me this? Why
not Nicolas?" I demanded in bewilderment.

"He did not want to tell you until the plans were
final. He knows you're in a state of nerves already. The
message has just come through. We leave tonight".

I was still only half convinced that it was not some
kind of joke, but I collected some possessions from
my dressing room and handed the bag to Smoltzoff
who waited for me at the stage door.

We arrived at the flat to find Nicolas throwing a few
things into a suitcase and I began to reproach him for
not telling me of his plans.

"I wanted to be quite sure", he said. "I heard only
this evening that the van is calling for us at half-past
two in the morning. Nadia – believe me – it will be
wonderful to be free; to dance where and what we like.
We'll build up your strength again with good food".

It was strange to hear Nicolas so enthusiastic about
leaving the country he loved so much. I knew it must
be on my behalf, yet I was distressed and uncertain.
Many times, I had longed to leave this new Russia
which I found so difficult to understand. Now that the
chance was offered I did not want to go. I could think
only of the happy times I had known, of the dancers
who were my friends, and the great stages that made
the background of my life. I began to put forward ob-

jections.

"We shall never get away safely. No one is allowed to leave Russia without a permit". But Nicolas seemed to have a new confidence and decisiveness. He put an arm around my shoulders for a moment, and then released me.

"It is all arranged", he said. "You will see. Now go and get some sleep while I finish here. I'll wake you when it is time".

I could not sleep, but lay on my bed, fully dressed, my mind moving restlessly. Nicolas knew best, of course. Perhaps I was more ill than I knew. Perhaps he guessed how much I wanted to be reunited with my father, mother, and Nan.

For a moment, I thought only of the joy this would bring. Then my doubts returned. It seemed dreadful to be leaving Russia so stealthily. Wherever we were we would dance, of course, but remembering the previous visit to Europe I knew it would never be the same...

When at last Nicolas came to tell me the van was at the door, I was seized with terror and sadness.

"No, I don't want to go! Do not make me". Nicolas soothed me. I was ill, he said; had never been strong. The situation might get worse.

"Come", he said, "it is all arranged".

Against this new firm manner, I seemed to have no defence. I allowed him to lead me to the van, but I sat huddled on the hard seat, utterly miserable.

We jogged through the quiet streets of Moscow in

the early morning and presently stopped at a railway siding, surround by open country. Here a hospital train was waiting and as we stumbled through the darkness towards the last carriage a man in a while coat motioned the three of us inside. Three beds were strung like hammocks from the roof.

"Get settled, quickly", whispered the man – apparently a doctor – "No one but myself knows that you are not really patients. Lie still, and in the morning a nurse will be along to take your temperatures".

The situation seemed so unreal that I felt it must all be a dream. A little calmer now, I lay in the hammock, too exhausted even to think.

Presently I became aware that Nicolas and Smoltzoff were whispering together uneasily.

"Something must have happened", I heard Nicolas say. "We were told we should be off at once".

When I realised that the train had not begun to move I sat up, gazing at the other two in apprehension.

"Oh, why did I let you make the attempt? If we stay here we shall be arrested!"

"It will be all right", said Nicolas but I noticed that he glanced out the darkened window, almost as if he expected my words to come true.

Smoltzoff was young and optimistic. He said cheerfully, "It's no good worrying, in any case, it is too late. Oh, the cakes you are going to buy me when we reach a shop that actually has some".

For three days, the train remained in the siding without moving. A nurse came three times a day to take our temperatures, or bring us meagre portions of food, but for most of the time we were alone. I became more nervous. Playing cards to pass the time, I lost continuously to the other two.

"That's two hundred and fifty cakes you owe me now", Smoltzoff informed me cheerfully.

I was too worried to enter into the joke. "The three days for which I signed off are already gone", I fumed. "Someone will be coming to look for me. I know they will". Smoltzoff had his doctor's certificate and Nicolas was not expected at regular theatre performances when he was working on a new ballet. Only I would be suspect, and I felt responsible. In my agitated state, I thought it might be a good idea to request extra leave.

That evening, after dark, I slipped away and running to the road, got a lift to the nearest telephone. As soon as the Director's voice boomed back at me, I doubted the wisdom of my move.

"I am not feeling well", I explained in a trembling voice. "Can I have another day or two of leave?"

I heard him laugh, "Poor child. Don't sound so scared. We'll send a doctor along to see what is wrong with you". "No, don't send a doctor!"

He must have heard the panic in my voice. "Certainly, we shall", he said sternly. "If he finds that you are shamming you will be taken to the theatre – and fined".

I dropped the receiver and thumbed a lift back to

the railway siding. Nicolas was wandering about, looking for me, and I threw myself into his arms and gabbled out my tale.

"How stupid I am!" I finished miserably. "Now they will be suspicious. Oh Kolia, I'm sorry".

Nicolas was so relieved at my safe return that he did not reproach me as he might have done. I was not to worry, he insisted. The Director could not have known from where I telephoned, and to these people on the train we were only numbers.

In spite of his comforting words, I passed a wakeful night, feeling sick with worry. Suddenly my heart missed a beat and I sat up in excitement. The train gave a jerk, men shouted, chains clanked and squeaked. Then the wheels began to turn. We were off.

I woke Nicolas and Smoltzoff to tell them the good news, and we exchanged delighted glances. At last – at last we were on our way to freedom!

With many delays and stops, the train crawled slowly southward. Thankful for every mile we covered, we three fugitives fell comfortably into the dull routine of the hospital train. Without protest, we swallowed the weak soup which had bits of fat floating on the top, took pills or aperients when they were offered and tried to seem like the invalids we were supposed to be. Stiff and bored, I sometimes cleared a space and, with a wary eye open for an unexpected visit from the nurse, insisted on a dancing lesson with Nicolas.

We seemed to have been travelling forever when

at last the train stopped at what was evidently a large station. Other trains could be heard, porters shouted, doors banged. I drew the curtains aside and glanced out, reading the name on the board.

"Kharkof, oh, Kolia!"

I gave a gasp and drew back sharply. From the windows of another train level with ours, I had seen the faces of two men who seemed to be regarding me with unusual interest. I had glimpsed the black-and-yellow badge of the Cheka – then the Secret Police!

When I told Nicolas, he laughed at my fears, but I was so certain we were discovered that I was already braced for the shock when the door of our carriage was flung open and the same two men I had seen addressed us by our names.

"We have been sent to bring you back with us to Moscow", they told us sternly.

I glanced at Nicolas in consternation and fear, and one of the men put his hand on my arm, speaking more gently. "Do not be frightened, Madame. We shall not hurt you". I shivered. "When we get back, we shall be punished, I suppose?"

Nicolas began to explain that it was on my account that he had arranged the escape.

"My wife is not well", he said. "I will come back with you to Moscow if you will just let her go – don't upset her, please".

The men listened to him with something like sympathy, then one of them said:

"We must carry out our orders, or we shall get into trouble. But listen, M. Lunatchasky, the Superintendent of Education, is visiting Kharkoff at the moment, and I've heard that he's a decent, understanding sort of chap. We could take you to him, if you like, and you can tell him what you've just told us".

"Lunatschasky!" I gasped, glancing at Nicolas with renewed hope. "You remember – he's Lydia's brother-in-law. If we could persuade him to write a letter to the theatre, explaining why we left, they might accept it. Lydia always said he has great influence". "I'll go and see him", said Nicolas. I pushed him aside. "No, *I'll* go. If I hadn't telephoned the theatre this would never have happened. It's *my* fault. Besides", I laughed nervously, "a woman is sometimes better at this sort of thing".

Leaving his confederate in charge of Nicolas and Smoltzoff, the other man escorted me to the interview.

The Superintendent's brother had coached me in some ballet roles. I knew from Lydia that the two brothers, though enemies in politics, were nevertheless friendly in private life. This made me feel that M. Lunatschasky must be a tolerant man.

He was charming to me and said he would write the letter if I would tell him what to say.

"You had better go back to your husband and talk it over", he told me. "When you have composed a suitable letter, I will sign it for you".

As I thanked him, he smiled and patted my shoulder. "You must not run away again", he said indulgently. "We cannot spare you. In any case, I insist that you dance for us here in Kharkoff tonight".

I went back to Nicolas and the three of us put our heads together to compose a letter which should soften the hearts of the authorities. In it, we explained that the husband and friend of this poor little dancer had only wanted to get her away to a place where she could rest and eat nourishing food. It was just a foolish impulse…

"And then", Nicolas said thoughtfully, sucking the end of the pencil, "We'll say that he thinks you *do* need a holiday, that he recommends it". "You wouldn't dare", said Smoltzoff, staring at Nicolas, while I added fearfully: "He won't sign the letter if you put that, Kolia. I'm sure he won't".

But my husband had his way and M. Lunatchasky signed without even reading the letter through! The three of us danced that night at Kharkoff's biggest theatre and we were given a great ovation. The Superintendent applauded from his box and came round afterwards to present flowers and tell me he was making arrangements for some further performances.

"I am determined not to give you up just yet", he said, wagging a finger at me. "I shall see to it that everything is settled amicably with the Bolshoi authorities".

We were in high spirits as we went back to the hotel where accommodation had been arranged for us.

"There's certainly more food to be had here", said Smoltzoff, glancing greedily into a shop window which had a display of cakes. "Don't forget, Nadia. You owe me two hundred and fifty!"

"I'll buy them for you tomorrow morning", I promised.

The next day we set off gaily for the baker's shop, and Smoltzoff sat down at once to consume his winnings. Egged on by Nicolas and me, he actually succeeded in demolishing fifty small cakes at one sitting!

We had a wonderful time in Kharkoff and were able to dismiss our fear of consequences. We felt that the Superintendent's letter must surely have had the desired result, or we should not have been allowed to stay on.

Arriving back in Moscow at last, we presented ourselves to the Director who informed us that he had decided, in view of the circumstances, to overlook our lapse. "But as M. Lunatchasky said, my wife is still far from well", Nicholas persisted, ignoring my warning frown. "I should like your permission to take her away for a holiday".

"We'll see what can be arranged", was the answer.

While I was waiting for the verdict on my case, I worked with Nicolas on a project for reforming the Moscow State Ballet School. The results created interest and approval and did much in our favour. Getting permission for leave of absence was, however, a long and tedious business and if it had not been for Nicolas's insistence, I would have given up. I was examined by one doctor after another and appeared before many committees and sub-committees. At last it was agreed that, subject to the confirmation of one more committee and the signatures of five important party Communists to guarantee our return, Nicolas and I would both be given a permit to go abroad for six months.

I was relieved that Nicolas could come, too. Privately I thought his own health in some question. He was an inveterate smoker, and when cigarettes became difficult to obtain he rolled his own with ordinary paper and any tobacco he could manage to get hold of. The result was an almost incessant cough, which worried me more than it did him.

The signatures for our permits were at last secured and the great day of the final confirmation found me sitting with several others on a hard bench in a great bare room. At a table sat twenty or more high officials who awaited the arrival of the Chief Commissar. Naked except for a hospital overall, hungry and shivering with cold, I longed for yet feared the coming of this important person who was to have the last word on my case. Hours passed in miserable apprehension, then at last there was a stir among the people who guarded the door, and the Commissar came in.

In spite of my discomfort and fear, I could scarcely keep from laughing. The man I had dreaded to meet was a large, very tall sailor, dressed in the traditional bellbottomed trousers and tunic with a square striped collar.

His tunic was open almost to the waist, showing a hairy chest, over which hung a string of enormous beads, like a mayoral chain. His cap was perched jauntily on the back of his head and a cluster of dark curls fell over his forehead. On his thick fingers were some fine rings.

He seemed like some figure from my stage world. Striding across the room, he took his seat at the table and when it became my turn to parade before him, he gave me a swift shy glance.

"Certainly, Comrade", he said. "You and your husband have my permission to go abroad for six months".

I thanked him and turned away, the papers of authority at last in my hands. Though this had been my desire for so long, I could not fight off a sense of depression. Should we ever come back to Russia?

CHAPTER EIGHT

Nicolas never cared a great deal for wealth. When he had money, he gave generously and liked to live well, but shoes were his only real extravagance. Now, however, with most of our possessions confiscated and no chance to accumulate money during our prolonged tours, we had few resources with which to finance our exit from Russia. We should need plenty if we were to fulfil our ultimate plan, which was to get to England. When I became depressed about it, Nicolas declared he would find a diamond which should provide our capital. "Don't laugh", he said cheerfully. "Remember the looting that went on and the valuable things which were thrown about".

Naturally, I scoffed at such an idea. A friend of my family – a Judge – lent us a little money but as he was only awaiting his own opportunity of leaving Russia, he could not spare much.

Nicolas developed what seemed to me an exasperating habit of walking along the streets with his gaze on the ground; looking, he asserted, for the diamond. One day, not long before the date we had fixed for our departure, we were hurrying down the Nevsky prospect in the rain when Nicolas stopped so suddenly that I almost fell over him.

"Look there!" he exclaimed. "Surely that is my diamond?"

The deep cracks in the pavement were full of rainwater, and I could certainly see something gleaming, but I was unprepared for Nicolas to fall on his knees and begin to poke about in the puddle with a stick. I tugged at him in embarrassment.

"Kolia – come away. It is just a piece of glass. Everyone is looking at you".

He took no notice but went on trying to poke the shining object out of the crack. A few people were beginning to gather round in curiosity, and I flounced away, saying: "I shall walk on, Kolia. You can look foolish by yourself"

I was almost at the end of the street when Nicolas came running up to me.

"It *is* a diamond, Nadia", he declared, displaying a small bright object on the palm of his hand. "I told you I would find one".

Still I scoffed, but he hurried me off to a jeweler friend who confirmed the find and offered a price for the diamond. I marvel even now at this fantastic piece of luck.

We left Russia with two other dancers who had been given leave of absence: Lola Lukoma and Boris Shavroff. With a violinist and a pianist to accompany the four of us, we gave concerts wherever we could get a booking, travelling slowly through Latvia and Lithuania and across the Baltic Sea to Sweden. At this point Lola and Boris began to be concerned about going back, and when Nicolas and I broke the news that this had never been our intention, we parted. We had no close relatives in Russia to worry about, as they had.

Nicolas and I arrived at last in Berlin where I made enquiries at the Embassy and discovered that my brother, Vladimir, was now with UFA films and still working in the city. We arranged a reunion, but for me it was only a prelude to the greater one I was longing for.

Vladimir

"Father and Mother – Nan – they're still in England?" I asked my brother as soon as our first excited greeting was over.

Mother and Father

"Yes. They're with Olga. How much do you know? Have you heard that the Anglo-Baltic Company was dissolved? Since then Father has had several jobs; the latest, I believe is with Cooks' as an interpreter". For a stricken moment, I contemplated the ruin of my brilliant father's career. But at least he was safe and well.

I was impatient to leave Berlin, but first we must not go empty-handed. It was not until the New Year that we were able to make our way to England. The family met us at Victoria station and at first, I did not recognise the little group under the clock; my father seemed to have shrunk and was in shabby civilian clothes instead of his splendid naval uniform. Mother looked older, and surely, that tall serious little girl couldn't be Nan! Nicolas had already recognised her. He darted forward to catch her in his arms, and a moment later we were

Nan

all laughing and crying together, not caring who saw us. In the taxi, we held hands and I could see the busy London streets only dimly through misty eyes. There was another reunion at the house in Golders Green, this time with my sister, Olga, and her husband. We sat up half the night talking, while my mother poured continually from the teapot, as she had done when presiding over the samovar in the old days. "I dreamed about you, Nadia", Olga told me. "I dreamed of you all one night, and then in the morning there was a letter! It was the one you wrote just before you left Russia".

"I never thought it would get to you", I confessed. "Oh, what a time you must have had in the South! I'm so thankful".

We had, indeed, much to be thankful for. Nan and I gazed at each other, half shyly, and it seemed strange that we must begin again to build up a relationship. My father spoke cheerfully of the various jobs with which he had tried to earn a living; the one with Cooks had already terminated, it appeared, owing to his habit of arguing with taxi-drivers and hotelkeepers about prices on his clients' behalf. Now he was employed as a property agent.

In spite of his jocular manner, my heart ached for him. They had made him a nobody now, I reflected bitterly; this brilliant man who had always loved and served his country well. But I couldn't let such thoughts spoil this first evening. I told them about some of our own experiences, and Nicolas chipped in, making light of the hardships, and amusing everyone with his graphic descriptions.

Though the trials of the past could be put behind us, the future had to be faced. Again, we had very little money, and we had to live. Nicolas and I discussed the situation in detail daily. What should we do now? How to insert ourselves in the dancing world of this our adopted country? We began to make enquiries as to how best to take up our chosen work again.

It was not easy to gain a footing. English people's concern for the plight of Russian refugees had long passed its peak, and some were already ensconced in a firm niche. Many knew us by reputation, however, and others became interested in us. The celebrated critic J.T. Grein wrote an article in the illustrated London News of March 10th, 1923, in which he described his visit to a small hall in Cricklewood where we, who had formerly danced in the splendour of the Imperial Theatres, gave an audition.

"I found here in obscurity", he wrote, "two of the greatest dancers alive. London cannot allow such artists to remain unknown. For Legat and Nicolaeva are destined to shine in London as they did in pre-war days in Moscow and St. Petersburg".

When Mrs. Benjamin Guinness gave a lavish party at her home – Sunningdale Park – she engaged us with a company of dancers to perform "Lac des Cygnes" in the open air. It was a warm summer evening and the beautifully kept grounds made an ideal setting for a splendid and artistic occasion. The dancers appeared from the woods beside the lake, and performed on specially constructed rafts, which floated on the water. Musicians played softly from boats moored among the reeds, and real swans swam gracefully in the background.

Many London papers reported on the occasion in the most glowing terms. The Daily Express of June 18th, 1923, gave it a long paragraph entitled "Fete Nocturne" which read: "...could one desire more than Nadine Nicolaeva (who scored a big success), Nicolas Legat, Novikoff, and the corps de ballet, giving to perfection the beautiful "Lac des Cygnes" while real swans watched them? It was a poem of motion".

We opened a studio in the Euston Road. Besides the ordinary rank and file of pupils, many famous dancers, hearing that the Maestro from the Maryinsky was available again came to us for class or private lessons: Idzikowsky, Lopokova, Algeranoff, Ninette de Valois, and many others. Mrs. Hoffman brought her 'girls' and Astafieva sent us Anton Dolin, a young man for whom she had great hopes. We were again launched.

In Russia Nicolas had spent many years teaching dancers who were dedicated and single minded in their attitude to their Art. He simply could not understand or have patience with the lesser type of pupil. Obstinately himself, he did not try very hard to learn the English language and would often poke fun, in Russian, at a tiresome pupil, secure in the knowledge that they could not understand.

"Kolia, stop it", I would chide him as, with a blithe smile, he hurled an insult at a poor unfortunate.

A shrug from him, a wave of the slender hands, a grin. "Even if she understood, this one would never believe", he retorted in Russian. "So stupid is she".

When he did essay a phrase in English, it had usually a humorous twist. "Your football must be Oxford Street" for "Your feet must be straight"; or "You may a little bit Leicester Square", when he wanted the pupils to relax and walk about for a while. (He never allowed a pupil to sit during a break).

It transpired that pupils for whom Nicholas had

Anton Dolin

only slight hopes were passed to me. Even in the Imperial School, I had discovered a flair for teaching such people. To wrestle with those pupils who were keen but a trifle dense could be rewarding, and to go back to their beginnings and discover where faults had begun provided a challenge. And improvement was a triumph. But it was to Nicolas, especially, that Seraphina Astafieva sent Anton Dolin. We were delighted to discover that she had made the most of the start we gave to her on our previous visit to England, and that her tuition was now sought after. She recognised Dolin's possibilities and thought he should now have some male tuition. "Pat", as he was then known to us, worked hard with Nicolas and adored him. Nicolas called him "Piccadilly" and it was some time before Pat realised this was a reference to the Eros statue, which Nicholas thought he resembled.

To our studio one day came a father with his little girl. The child was about twelve years of age, shy and pale, with a pixie-shaped face, large dark eyes and very thin legs. She was Alicia Marks, later to be known all over the world as the great Alicia Markova. Nicolas realised she had great promise and she became one of his favourite pupils.

Teaching alone, however, was not enough for us. We formed a small company of our own called the Moscow Art Dancers, performing in many West End and provincial theatres. Nicholas developed a touch of neuritis in his arm at this time and supporting and lifting took a great deal out of him. "Pat", who was practising partnering work with me, seemed to possess unusual ability and intuition, and now I suggested he should substitute for Nicholas in a pas de deux at the London Palladium where we were due in September. As Anton Dolin, he took part in this programme and danced a solo, but his pas de deux with me was his first in public with a ballerina. The occasion made a great impression on him, and though his inexperience gave me some bad moments in rehearsals, my belief that he would one day be an exceptional partner was on the way to being justified.

Little Alicia Marks was also a member of our company, and we had to obtain a special license for her to appear as she was underage. She danced a solo called "The Dragonfly", an easier version of her own favourite that, when she demonstrated it to Nicolas, had in it thirty-two fouettes! He rearranged it in a more suitable manner for so immature a dancer.

Audiences loved "Little Alicia" and she received some good notices in the press. One paper, however, made the guarded comment: "She is too young for anyone to give a really firm opinion of her future…" I wonder if that critic remembered his words.

In any case, Alicia enjoyed it all immensely, and no adult could have been a better trouper. Her license forbade her to dance after nine o'clock and once, when

Alicia Markova
Photo Courtesy of Tasha Bertram

the programme was running over its time and it looked as though her own dance might be cancelled, she ran on to the stage before Susan May – an older dancer – had finished her solo.

"Go back!" ordered Susan. But Alicia pretended not to hear. She tried to fit her own dance into the music and the two of them were whirling round each other, much to the older girl's annoyance.

I was amused by the little incident and felt it to be added proof of my belief that this child would one day reach the goal of stardom which she had so obviously set for herself. How right I was! Soon after this her dancing came to the notice of Serge Diaghilev himself and she joined his famous company as its most junior member going on from strength-to-strength throughout the years.

In December of 1924, Nicolas and I danced at the Princes Theatre in the yearly "Sunshine Matinee" for blind babies. Our presentation of "La Poupee" was by special request of the critic of the Dancing Times who had seen it earlier at the Palladium and thought our mime outstanding.

During the following year, we had many engagements and our studio became more popular. The background of my busy public life, however, contained several private worries. I was concerned about my father who had lost yet another job through his innate but unwelcome honesty and nonconformity. Now he needed an operation. I hated, also, to see my mother striving to cope with the domestic chores of our large household. Then there was the inability of Nicolas to fit into English

Legat Caricature

ways; the natural frustration resulting from a different attitude to our Art. And there was Nan. It did not take me long to discover that the unusual trials and experiences of her earlier childhood had left their mark upon Nan. From the first moment of our reunion she gave me a strong affection, but she was strangely locked up within herself, and often unhappy. I did not know how to help her.

Though she was not progressing as fast as we would like at the Convent School she attended, she wanted to learn ballet, and came almost every day to the studio for a lesson.

She showed great promise in spite of the big gap in her training, and we encouraged her to take minor parts in some of the shows we gave.

She greatly admired the Hoffman girls who, although they came to our studio for ballet, were really acrobats. Nan was forbidden to try their tricks, but I guessed that she did so when Nicolas and I were out of the way. I was terrified she would hurt herself. One day, trying to do somersaults in the air, she fell heavily on her back, and fainted. The Hoffman girls brought her round and were sworn to secrecy, but the next day Nan

Nan

could not get up and had to confess what happened. I sent for the doctor. He prescribed rest for a week, after which time Nan pretended that she was all right. I did not know until long afterwards that she suffered from backache almost continuously, and I could not understand why she was so listless, so difficult in many ways.

I began to feel again the need of some power beyond myself. With all the hard work, the alarms and hardships of the later years in Russia, my exploration into the realms of philosophy had been abandoned, though never forgotten. I could not talk to Nicolas about my longing to discover the meaning of life and death. Always he would say cheerfully: "We shall have plenty of time later to find out what happens when we are dead". Or, "God keeps us in darkness for our own good".

I accepted the fact that he felt differently, but for myself I needed to enquire. Now I could discuss such matters with my father who had always shared my interest. I rediscovered Yoga and took seriously the recommendations of certain Indian teachers.

"The exercises give me more control over my breathing, and I can dance longer without becoming exhausted". I told Nicolas. "It is right, I think, that we should eat less and drink more". "I thought you didn't drink?" mocked my husband. "Not spirits; water, or fruit juices. You are a tease, Kolia".

I heard that P. D. Ouspensky, the Russian philosopher, was in London and I began attending his lectures.

Ouspensky, a former Russian journalist, first met Gurdjieff in Moscow. He realised almost at once that

Nicolaeva

Gurdjieff had the kind of knowledge he had been seeking in vain, and the association developed. Later, when Ouspensky was a refugee and stranded in Constantinople, people who knew of his book "Tertium Onganum" invited him to London. Efforts were almost made to get Gurdjieff over from Paris to join him. Authority decided that there were already too many refugees in England, and Gurdjieff remained in Paris to establish in a Fontainebleu chateau the Institute for the Harmonious Development of Man, founded on his teaching. Later I was fortunate in being asked to visit him there.

Ouspensky himself was a short thickset man with close-cropped hair and strong glasses; not the usual conception of a philosopher. Studying with him, however, began a new development of my mind. I found his theories fascinating and became friendly with him and his wife, who often invited me to their house.

I made another effort to interest Nicolas, and to please me he came to one or two lectures. For a while, he would sit quietly, then begin playing some childish trick, or mimic the lecturer until those around him were stifling their laughter. It was not only distracting, it was embarrassing, and at length I would make some excuse to leave. Once outside, Nicolas was cheerful and unrepentant.

"Now let's go and have something to eat", he would suggest with an air of great relief. "I suppose it's all right if you like 'harmonious development', right thinking and all that sort of thing. I don't feel any urge in that direction, and I do not understand what they are talking about".

In a way, I envied Nicolas his simple, uncomplicated nature. He treated all my excursions into these matters with gentle contempt, and though sometimes, when I felt I *must* talk to him about it, he pretended to be interested, I knew that he secretly mocked my enthusiasm. If I looked thoughtful, or did not hear a question put to me, he would tiptoe to my side and whisper: "Are you on the fifth plane now? Surely you should have reached the seventh?"

I would not allow him to turn me aside. Throughout the rest of my life, the philosophies and religions of the world have continued to hold a strange fascination for me.

Dances of the Past "The Pavane" circa 1925
Nicolaeva and Nicolas

Nicolaeva and Nicolas
Jewish Wedding Dance

Mazurka

CHAPTER NINE

My family had never lost touch with Miss Ward. We were delighted to meet her again and talked to her about Nan, with the result that "Missy" came to live with us. Nan was pleased and seemed brighter. She was getting on well with her dancing, though she tired easily and was inclined to be a little stiff, especially when performing grands battements. However, the doctor could find nothing wrong. She was growing fast, he said, and it would be best not to press her too hard.

During 1924, our little company gave many successful shows, and Nicolas and I danced pas de deux at several charity balls. Nicolas was, of course, responsible for all the choreography. He also arranged a ballet at Drury Lane. In this year too, my father had a successful surgery, and we moved to a house in Highgate.

Agrippina Vaganova

We were working hard at the studio. Though the "Moscow Art Dancers" lost both Anton Dolin and the young Markova to Diaghilev, they came to us for lessons, as did many others in that company. For the Russian dancers in England the Legat Studio had a nostalgic quality. Here they could not only perfect their technique under the eye of one of the finest teachers in the world, but they could also gossip with us and each other, recalling the past glories of performances in the old Imperial Theatre of their homeland. There was no denying the fact that nothing here was on so grand a scale; even the Diaghilev ballets were mere ex-

tracts, often sand-wiched between other Music Hall items. We exiles thought often of those left behind to carry on the tradition of Russian ballet – a tradition that has never failed. Vaganova, who became Director of the Leningrad Ballet Company (once the Maryinsky) was, her-self, a pupil of Legat.

Coppelia

In the autumn of that year, Sir Oswald Stoll came to see The Moscow Art Dancers in one of their per-formances and booked the company for the London Coliseum and the Alhambra. At the former theatre we followed the Diaghilev season; a severe test but one which we came through well. Again, the scene from "Coppelia" with Nicolas Legat and Nadeja Nicolaeva gained the critics' special praise and attention.

In Russia, one of my specialties had been "La Mort du Cygne", arranged for me by Nicolas. In England this dance was now associated with Pavlova, though actually the two dances were quite different. I danced "The Swan" at the Alhambra, and the usual comparisons were made; one newspaper speaking of "Nicolaeva, comparable with the hitherto incomparable Pavlova", while another asserted firmly that I had "the greatest technique of the present day". If that were so, it was because I had the benefit of the greatest teacher of the day.

The Swan

In the early spring of 1925, Serge Diaghilev was in a dissatisfied mood. Since that most brilliant male dancer - Nijinsky - was stricken with illness, it seemed that no one had been able to take his place in the great Impresario's affections with any degree of permanence. Massine was in favour for a time, but there was disagreement. Then, there was a Spanish boy, and later Anton Dolin who as an individualist was already finding the stranglehold unwelcome.

I was having a lesson with Nicolas one day at the studio when the door opened, and Diaghilev came in. His heavily built figure topped with a massive head and bulging brow like that of a lion, seemed to dwarf his young companion. Serge Lifar was then an attractive youth with large brown eyes, silky black hair and a soft mouth.

I used to say that he might have been taken for an Italian or a Spaniard, but Nicolas insisted that his snub nose made him obviously a Russian. (Later he had an operation on his nose which altered his appearance slightly).

"I have brought Serge to you", Diaghilev told Nicolas, swinging his stick with a studied carelessness that could not mask the seriousness of his intention, "because I'd like your opinion of his dancing capabilities. I think something more could be made of him".

Nicolas nodded at Lifar and took up the fiddle he still used at times to accompany his pupil's steps. "Show me what you can do", he said.

When Lifar had changed into his practise clothes, he moved at Diaghilev's instruction, into the centre of the room. The young dancer seemed nervous, and to help him regain his composure, I turned my back on him and began some exercises. When I glanced round, I saw that he was copying me faithfully.

Nicolas said he would test Lifar's elevation. He sat at the piano and struck several chords, ordering Lifar to jump higher and higher. At the finish, Nicolas turned to Diaghilev, and nodded again. "He *could* be very good, I think".

Diaghilev gave a satisfied smile. "What did I say? Look, Nicolai, I'll release Serge from his rehearsals for a bit so that he can have a private lesson with you every day. Agreed? Make him work. I want quick results".

Nicolas took a great deal of trouble with Lifar, working with him patiently each day. The boy began to show improvement; so much so that a critic of performances in that season of Russian Ballet at the Coliseum mentioned Lifar as one of three who were emerging as stars...

"I'm going off with the Company for a short season in Spain and Paris, but during the holidays I intend taking Serge with me to Italy. It will be – an education for him". He paused. "If you and Nadia care to come along as well he can continue his lessons with you at the same time".

As always, he expected only to speak, and the thing was as good as done. I could see that the idea of a holiday in Italy appealed to Nicolas and that unless I intervened he would consent without further thought. "We shall have to talk it over", I said. "Shan't we Kolia?"

When Diaghilev had gone, I put my objections. I pointed out to Nicolas that our dancing reputation in England was gaining strength, and our studio becoming more popular. "I think we shall lose ground as we did before, if we leave it to others", I said. "Besides, how much is his holiday going to cost us?"

Even Nicolas could see that this was an important question. My father was now unemployed and frail in health. Remembering how Olga and her husband had bolstered the family finances when we were in Russia, I wanted to do my share. Could we afford to risk a niche that had been so hardly won?

We talked it over with my father, who had become our business manager. With his clear head for figures, his advice was invaluable. In the end, Diaghilev went off to the Continent without the answer he sought. Though I, too, longed for the sunshine and warmth of Italy, I put the matter from my mind. Two months later, however, a telegram arrived from Diaghilev, already in Italy. He renewed his offer and demanded an immediate decision.

As Nicolas handed me the slip of paper he made a little grimace, then sighed. "I suppose we must refuse, but, it should be nice in Italy now…"

I read the telegram again and hesitated. The financial commitments in

Diaghilev, Lifar, Boris Kochno and Danilova

England were mostly on my side of the family. Had I any right to refuse Nicolas something he so evidently wanted? Besides, a holiday would do him good. I was still worried about his cough, and about the dizzy feelings of which he complained sometimes.

"Let's go", I said. "It isn't for long. Surely people can do without us for a while".

The next few days were exhausting; making the necessary arrangements for our substitutes and packing. When we left London, however, it was a cool grey morning that made us congratulate ourselves on our decision. It would be a pleasant change to see blue skies.

Arriving at the station in Venice, hot and tired after our journey we found Serge Lifar waiting to give us a heartening welcome. Alexandra Trusevitch and Boris Kochno, the secretaries, accompanied him. As we made our way down to the quayside, I found myself thinking that it was all rather like some stage setting; the wide canal sparkling in the sunshine, the black gondolas, the policemen in their bright uniforms and wide hats. The sight of Diaghilev, massive

Serge Diaghilev

and brooding, sitting heavily at the far end of a nearby gondola, seemed to complete the illusion rather than dispel it. I was reminded of his dread of death by water, and wondered if here in Venice, it seemed closer. He roused himself to welcome us and as we glided along the canal, pointed out various places of interest. We looked suitably impressed, though both Nicolas and I had been in Venice before; he as a dancer, I as a little girl on holiday with my grandmother. We turned into a narrower waterway and stopped near the great square of St. Marks. As we got out, Lifar took Nicolas's arm and said again how glad he was that he had been able to come. Diaghilev broke in with an order.

"Serge, go on ahead to the café and reserve a table for us, not too near the music. We must all have some ice cream".

I noticed the hint of jealousy and made up my mind to warn Nicolas to be careful.

Presently we left Diaghilev and Lifar together, and Alex escorted us to the pension where she had reserved a room for us.

She led the way out of the square and into a narrow dark turning where a dingy café displayed a faded awning. To my amazement, she entered, and we followed her to the back of the shop where a door opened on to a small courtyard. A steep flight of crumbling steps led up to a room above. I turned to Nicolas in dismay.

"Why do we have to stay here? I don't like the look of it at all. In any case I heard Diaghilev say the practice studio is on the other side, near the Lido".

"I know it isn't imposing, but the food is good", Alex said with an offended air. "We didn't think you would want to spend too much on accommodation".

I bit back a retort and followed her up. There were no rugs on the stone floor of the large shabby room and a huge iron bedstead, a clumsy washstand, and two chairs were the only furniture. I would have made a protest and left at once, but Nicolas frowned me into silence. When Alex had gone, he said soothingly: "Don't worry, Nadia, it will do for tonight. Tomorrow I'll speak to Diaghilev. Or perhaps I could find a room in a nice little villa somewhere near the Lido".

He looked so happy and optimistic that I said no more. Privately I thought Diaghilev had treated us shabbily. After persuading us to come to Italy, he might at least have seen that we had good accommodation.

By the bestowal of a large tip, we managed to get the slatternly maid to bring hot water, and after a wash and a change of clothes, we went out to meet Diaghilev again. I could not resist showing my disapproval of our quarters, but he only shrugged his great shoulders and smiled. He and Lifar were, of course, staying at the Grand Hotel together.

It was good, however, to see Nicolas in such good spirits. The sunshine and the warmth seemed to bring out the sense of fun which was always only just below the surface. Now, as we bought tickets for the boat that was to take us over to the Lido, he sank to his knees and peered over the barrier to ask in a high-pitched voice for a child's ticket. On board, he drew on a scrap of paper a comical sketch of Diaghilev as "Captain of the Ship"; this he gave to Alex saying that when he died it might be worth a great deal of money. Affected by his gaiety, I forgot my resentment and joined in the fun.

When we reached the Lido, Diaghilev conducted us to an old house which stood in neglected grounds at the end of a long drive. The entrance hall was spacious and contained a fine marble staircase; through an open doorway we saw a young man at work on a large painting. Diaghilev introduced us to Pruna, who had painted the scenery for "Les Matelots". Now he was working on a life-sized painting of Lifar. Diaghilev gazed at it in obvious admiration but to me it looked like a grotesque distortion. Catching sight of the look of Nicolas's face, I knew he was about to say something rude and I nudged him into silence.

Nicolaeva taking her lesson from Legat

Presently we all went out to a café. Lifar began to enumerate with relish the items on the menu, but Diaghilev reminded him rather curtly that he must watch his figure. Nicolas, seeing the look of frustration on the younger man's face, said gaily:

"You won't have to bother about dieting now. Training with me will keep down your weight. Just look at my poor little wife! There is scarcely anything of her".

I let the remark pass. It would have been unkind of point out that I ate very little and was a vegetarian by choice. I always tried not to put a damper on Nicolas's enjoyment of big meals. People are all different, the laws of nature varying with each individual! "What is good for a Russian can be death for a German!" as an old proverb points out. The next morning Nicolas set off early, returning in triumph to report that he had found a room to rent in a villa belonging to private residents. We went there at once. The room had a terrace overlooking a garden gay with flowers and as we stood there admiring the view Nicolas said happily: "I have been thinking out a new combination of steps for you, Nadia". He moved his fingers on the top of the balustrade, demonstrating; "See, pas de basque, sissone en tournant, fouette en dehors, tombe".

Of course, I had to kick off my shoes and try them and immediately we became absorbed. Every day we went to the practise room and Lifar and I worked until we were exhausted. Diaghilev encouraged Nicolas to give Lifar a good deal of partnering work, for I was easy to lift, and knew just how to distribute my weight in order to give the least strain. There was no piano, but Nicolas had brought his violin to Italy, and though some might not call it music, the rhythmic emphasis was perfect accompaniment for our dancing.

Diaghilev came often to watch and seemed pleased with Lifar's progress. He spoke again of Cecchetti's recent appointment as ballet master and director of the Scala Academy in Milan and reiterated his hope that Nicolas would take his place, both of us joining the Company. We had made our objections the first time and could only repeat them.

After our practice, we would go to a restaurant, or Lifar and I donned bathing suits and swam, together with Alex and Boris. The relationship between these two was always something of an enigma. It had been said that they were in love; others ridiculed such an idea. One thing about our stay in Italy was evident. Lifar was never to be on his own.

A few days after our arrival, Diaghilev told Nicolas that there was to be a big party at which Lifar and I would dance. He went on to say that he had arranged for us to practise on the stage of the small theatre which was now closed for the summer. Sokolova and Woizikowsky, who were passing through Venice, were to be included in the programme.

"I thought", he finished, "that Serge might dance 'La Spectre de la Rose'."

I saw Nicolas frown. Never, in his dealings with Diaghilev, could he conform to the convention that one must not argue with the great man. Now he said that it was a pity in his opinion, to keep repeating the same well-known extracts.

"Why not let me arrange something new", he finished. To my surprise, Diaghilev made no objection. Later, when we separated and Nicolas and I were on our way to our modest lodgings, I said: "That was a triumph for you Kolia. I did not think you could get your way so easily".

Nicolas smiled. "Did you not tell me to be tactful? What I really meant was that "Spectre de la Rose" is still too closely connected with Nijinsky, and Lifar is not ready for it yet".

"We shall celebrate your tact in ice cream!" I said gaily.

Nicolas worked on the new pas de deux. He called it "Valse Caprice" and set it to the music of Rubenstein. Diaghilev approved the outline and when Lifar and I began to practise the dance, he attended all the sessions, making a criticism here, or a suggestion there.

On the night of the party, the Palazzo Papadopoli was brilliantly lit at every window, and along the wide drive passed a constant procession of carriages and cars. The highest society of Venice and the neighbouring countryside was invited and a crowd of sightseers waited at the gates to peer at each new arrival and whisper comments. Nicolas and I drove up in a hired carriage and as I mounted the steps leading to the magnificent entrance, I carried my white ballet dress carefully in my arms so that it should not be creased.

My dressing room was banked with flowers and sumptuous, but I scarcely noticed. As always, I was nervous before the performance. Undressing, I pulled on my silk tights, then dropped over my head the white chiffon dress; the skirts caught up at intervals with tiny bunches of blue forget-me-nots, a garland of the same flowers to encircle my hair.

As I walked slowly down the wide staircase into the hall where the performance was to be given, I was aware of the splendid audience; the ripple of anticipation. Then, as the music of "Valse Caprice" began, I forgot my surroundings and saw only Lifar, my partner. We slid easily into the teasing retreats and hesitations of the dance which culminated in a final coming-together. Poised high in Lifar's arms, I could see Diaghilev in the corner, his big head nodding at me in satisfaction and as the applause rang out I felt a four-fold pleasure; for him, for Lifar, for myself and for my husband who created the roles.

Yet when I was again in my dressing room and changing into the "Swan" costume an immense depression swept over me.

"Why do you always want me to dance this?" I asked Nicolas almost angrily. "You know there is always the comparison…"

Nicolas patted my hand. "You are dancing it because it is one of your best. Also, there are people here who know you and have requested it. Come, do you not remember that time in Russia when you danced "The Swan" in Norwegian dress, because the audience would not be satisfied without it, even though you were not prepared?" As always, Nicolas was able to make me laugh. The tension was eased, and I was ready to face the audience again.

It was only a few days after this that Diaghilev suddenly told us we should be going to Florence the following morning. I was somewhat disturbed by the abrupt announcement for I was expecting letters from home and chafed at the delay a forwarding address would cause.

When I walked down to the post-office that afternoon, however, it was to find a long letter from my father. Seemingly, all was well with the family and with the studio. Putting doubts from my mind I gave myself up to the enjoyment Florence was sure to bring.

CHAPTER TEN

In Florence, Diaghilev went around the museums and galleries with Lifar as though they were schoolmaster and pupil. Nicolas always begged to be excused from such excursions, while I preferred to wander about on my own, gazing at the graceful buildings and fine statues, or visiting the libraries to see the rare and choice books.

All too soon, we left for Rome. Here again Diaghilev went off with Lifar to the best hotel, leaving us to find what other accommodation we could. We had, however, became used to his ways and liked to be on our own. Remembering those dependent on us, we usually found a small hotel for bed and breakfast, eating out at cheap restaurants to save money.

It was the first time I had been in Rome and I was impressed by the Holy City, but Nicolas remained unaffected by my enthusiasm and was content to lounge about while I went off to sit under the great dome of St. Peter's, or stroll through the Forum and contemplate the ruins of the Coliseum. The visit was again too short for me, and it was with feelings of frustration that I learned Diaghilev had decreed we should move south to Naples, Capri, and Sorrento. However, Diaghilev was in an unusually expansive mood. At the hotel, he ordered dinner for all of us and it was obvious that no expense was to be spared. There were many delicious courses, and the meal finished with a dish of roasted grapes; fresh-picked fruit sewn up inside their own leaves with thread, and then put into the oven. Pulled from the fork, the grapes were deliciously saturated in juice.

Nicolas embarked on one of his amusing anecdotes. Lifar, sitting next to Diaghilev and laughing with his mouth full of grapes, choked uncontrollably. Juice spurted out of his mouth, spattering in all directions. Diaghilev drew away from him, slowly wiping his face.

"Serge – behave yourself", was all he said, but it was obvious that this small incident had ruined his good mood; Lifar looked quite stricken as he muttered his apologies.

I marveled, as always, at Diaghilev's complete lack of facial expression. Only his eyes showed when he was interested, amused, or angry. Yet his personality was so strong that he imposed his moods on all around him.

After coffee, he rose abruptly, motioning Lifar to follow him, and we saw them no more that night. Nicolas and I went with the other diners into an adjoining hall where there was to be a conjuring performance. A small pale-faced man emerged on to the platform and fidgeted nervously with the props on the table. When we were all seated, he produced a pack of cards and gabbling some rather feeble patter swept them through the air in an effort to make them disappear. Several of them fell to the floor at the first attempt, and even when he tried again, the effect was not quite as it should be. Nicolas, sitting beside me in the front row, laughed loudly and clapped his hands together with mock enthusiasm. The little conjuror must have sensed the mockery, for he suddenly held out of the cards, saying in a somewhat sarcastic voice: "Perhaps the gentleman would like to try?"

Nicolas had drunk just a little too much wine. He leaped to his feet at the challenge, and though I tried to pull him back, he was on the platform in a moment. He not only made the cards disappear more expertly, but also discovered them again in the pockets of the first performer. To the sound of cheers and applause from the audience, Nicolas made his way back jauntily to his seat. I shook my head at him.

"That was mean of you, Kolia", I whispered. "You have spoiled the poor little man's reputation". He threw me a comically contrite expression, saying, "I did not mean to. I promise to sit quietly for the rest of the performance".

When the feeble show was over and the conjuror came round with the collection plate, I saw Nicolas drop in a hundred lire note with a "will-that-absolve-me?" air. I was much amused when afterwards the conjuror waylaid Nicolas to suggest, in all seriousness, that the two of them should set up in partnership!

On our way to Rome by train, Diaghilev was sitting next to Nicolas. I caught a stray word or two of the conversation, and realised that Diaghilev was again expressing the hope that we would change our minds and join his Company after all. I was scarcely disturbed, for Nicolas and I had talked it over so often and come to the same conclusion each time. I returned my attention to my book and became absorbed.

When we collected our letters on arrival, there was another from my father. I sat down at once in our hotel room to read it.

"People are saying that you have joined up with Diaghilev for good", he wrote. "Some of the pupils are talking about leaving. I do beg you to think carefully over the possible consequences of such a decision…"

There was more of a slightly worrying nature; money difficulties, some little trouble with Nan – I folded the letter thoughtfully, inclined to blame myself for leaving others to cope with everything; for enjoying this holiday so much.

I glanced at Nicolas. "We must go back to England at once", I told him. He looked startled. "Why? What has happened?" When I told him, what my father had written he made a wry face. "I've just told Diaghilev we will join up with him". "But Kolia – why? We agreed …"

"Well – you see he has promised you some good parts". He paused, then hurried on: "And he wants me to produce new ballets. I was sure I could persuade you to agree. After all, we shall both be earning. There's more in it than just teaching".

I could guess what it meant to Nicolas to have the chance of arranging ballets for a larger company again. For myself, too, it would be a treat to dance in more lavish productions than our own little company could manage. Ought I to try and reverse his decision?

With a sense of panic, I turned it over in my mind. We would, as Nicolas pointed out, be earning, while the studio would go on. As to Nan, her grandmother had had more to do with her upbringing than I. She would surely know what to do. "If you've already given your word", I began.

That was enough for Nicolas. He swept me up into his arms and balanced me high above his head, just for the fun of it. Then he set me down. "Don't worry about the family", he said gaily. "We shall be going to London soon for the Coliseum season and we can straighten everything out then. Come, you must drink to our new venture, if only in lemon-

Have Joined the Diaghileff Company.
Nadejda Nicolaeva and Nicolas Legat, the well-known teachers and dancers, have now joined the Diaghileff Company, and will be appearing in some of the ballets at the Coliseum. They are here seen in a Norwegian Character Dance.

ade!"

A day or so later Diaghilev went on ahead to Paris, leaving us to follow with Lifar. But he forgot the question of money, and we were forced to borrow a part of the fare from a friend who happened to be in Italy at that time.

It had been a splendid holiday, however. As to Lifar, I thought he had really appreciated our company and what Nicolas was able to do for him. Indeed, in later years he wrote of the holiday in one of his books saying, "My memory will always hold this trip as one of the most important happenings in my life; one that did most to foster my spiritual development".

In Paris, we joined up with other members of the Diaghilev Company. We knew them all, of course: Idizkowsky, Nemchinova, Sokolava, Danilova, Nikitina and the rest, including our former pupil Alicia Markova, the youngest member of the group. Grigoriev was the stage director. Anton Dolin was not with us. We knew that he was now dancing in revue and that he had opened his own school in England.

Rumour had it that Diaghilev's intention to give Serge Lifar roles that had hitherto been reserved for Dolin precipitated the break. How true that was I do not know, but I thought I sensed among the present company some jealousy of Lifar's position. I suspected also that because we had been for this holiday with Diaghilev, Nicolas and I were involved in it.

The rehearsals in Paris took place at a flat belonging to a dancing mistress. The large room had barres round the walls and attached to the heavier furniture, for it was also the living room; a tiny kitchen led off it, and here we constantly brewed coffee for our refreshment.

Nicolas, as ballet-master, became immediately engrossed in teaching. I did my best to fit into some sort of niche, but almost at once I could see that the new venture was going to prove something of a disappointment to me. I was to dance "Aurora's Wedding" and I could feel no enthusiasm for it.

"It's a mixture of "The Sleeping Beauty", "Casse Noisette", and "Lac des Cygnes", I complained to Nicolas. "A sort of Russian Salad!" Nicolas laughed and gave his characteristic shrug. "Yes, it is a shame. But no doubt, Diaghilev thinks audiences in Europe are not yet ready for full-length ballet. We saw that, ourselves, when we were in England".

This was true, of course, yet it sometimes seemed to me that Diaghilev was in a position to put his own popularity to the test and produce something with a more serious intention. I thought it was probably a question of finance. The extraordinary thing is that in the present-day people regard Serge Diaghilev with admiring reverence, yet at the time of which I am speaking, he did not have the support or the financial backing that such an attitude implies. Often he did not know where to turn for the money to keep his company going.

He was, undoubtedly, a clever forceful character,

though not, I am sure, a happy man. The complications of his possessive affections, his diabetic constitution and his fear of death would have precluded that. I remember that when we were in Paris he was confined to his room for a few days. Nicolas and I went to the hotel to enquire and he sent word for Nicolas to come up and see him. As I waited in the vestibule one of the dancers swept in, her arms laden with flowers, which she left at the desk with instructions for them to be taken immediately to Diaghilev's room. A few days later, when he appeared at rehearsals again, this same dancer went up to him, asking coyly: "Did you get my flowers?" He raised his monocle and gave her a grim look. "So, *you* were the fool who brought flowers!" he growled. "Flowers are for death – they even *smell* of death…"

As the rehearsals for what I called "ballet snippets" advanced, I began to see that Diaghilev was wise to attempt no more. To produce a classical ballet in its entirety one must have a team of the finest dancers all working harmoniously together. In this company, there was too much chopping and changing, and not enough artists with a truly advanced technique. I remembered, with nostalgia, the lavish and artistic productions on the great stages of the Imperial theatres of Russia, from which Nicolas and I were refugees.

There were Russian refugees of every sort in Paris now; people who had been nurtured in luxury now worked as film-extras, taxi-drivers, dance-hostesses, or even as washers-up in the big hotels. Again, and again, we came across old acquaintances from Petrograd or Moscow. In their leisure time, they sat in the open-air cafes making a cup of coffee or a glass of wine last for hours and reminding each other of more prosperous days.

Also, in Paris at this time was Sir Paul Dukes, my father's friend of long standing. He reminded me now that it was in 1912 that they first met; Paul having temporarily taken the place of a sick friend who was the English tutor at the Naval College.

Paul Dukes

"It was kind of the Admiral to notice me in those days", he commented. "He was so much older, so much more important, and my interest in music made me a poor teacher. I was amazed when I ran across him in London".

Paul came often to our room in Paris and one day, looking over my shoulder as I sat reading, he exclaimed: "I did not know you were interested in Yoga!" I smiled. "It is not so surprising. We have seldom met for long." It appeared that he, too, was fascinated by such teachings. We plunged into animated discussion, and I told him that I had studied with Ouspensky in London and that through this friendship Nicolas and I had been invited to spend the weekend at Chateau du Prieure, where Gurdjieff had his Institute.

"I envy you", said Paul. "You must remember everything and tell me about it when you come back".

The visit to Fontainebleu was certainly a strange experience. The Chateau had been a palace in Napoleon's time, and afterwards a monastery. Now it was given up to what Gurdjieff had called "The Harmonious Development of Man".

When we arrived, we were shown to our room by a woman who wore a preoccupied expression, and we passed other solitary and withdrawn individuals as we made our way downstairs to the large drawing room. Here Gurdjieff was sitting on a settee, cross-legged, with a small piano accordion on his lap. He nodded gravely as we entered, but did not speak; continuing to make weird, wailing sounds on the instrument while a man at the grand piano strummed an accompaniment.

I regarded Gurdjieff with interest. He was slightly Eastern in appearance, I thought, with heavy brows, and a large, greying moustache. His dark eyes had a merry look, and he smiled continually.

The sound of a gong interrupted the session and we followed the rest into another room, all standing behind our chairs on each side of a long refectory table. As soon as we were seated, and glasses of Armagnac had been passed round, Gurdjieff leaped to his feet and lifted his glass.

"Let us drink to the Idiots!" he cried. Everyone but myself sprang up to drink and repeat the toast. Gurdjeiff glanced at me, frowning. "Drink!" he commanded in Russian. "Drink the toast!" I shook my head. "I don't drink spirits", I said firmly. "I'm sorry. Will you excuse me?"

He frowned again but made no further comment. I sat there, bewildered, as members of the party jumped up again and again to toast the Idiots, Arch-Idiots, Double-Idiots and so on. I saw Nicolas glance at me with a comical shrug and I hoped he would remember the promise I had extracted from him: that he would keep his feelings to himself.

I learned afterwards that Gurdjieff first originated the toast in contempt of people who fawned upon him, regarding him as a sort of magician and hoping to see him perform all sorts of fakir tricks.

"People are lazy", he would say. "They come to me and ask: 'where shall I be at this time next year?' or 'what shall I do?' I tell them they must make up their own minds, where they want to be, what they wish to do. Perhaps then I can tell them how they may achieve their ambitions".

On the table were jars containing red peppers, pickled marrows, salted cucumbers and other preserves. I refused them all, saying they were too strong for my taste, and I could not be persuaded by the other guests to drink the fiery liqueur.

When the meal ended at last, Gurdjieff turned to me.

"Come!" he said in his lordly way.

I walked at his side through rooms richly carpeted and furnished, everyone else following in procession. We went by another door into a covered passage that led to a barnlike building adjoining the chateau. Here, too, the floors were spread with fine Oriental rugs and silk-covered cushions, a fountain in the centre spraying scented water. We all sat down on the cushions, facing a stage, while Gurdjieff mounted to an organ loft and began to play. As the strange monotonous music poured forth, the stage curtains drew back to reveal dancers in shapeless dresses of some soft white material, with wide sleeves like a kimono. Their heads were close-banded with scarves of the same cloth, so that one could scarcely tell whether they were male or female. They swayed, postured, and circled, their arms folded across their breasts, or moving languor- ously, and as they danced, they made a weird chanting or counted out-loud.

It was like no other dancing I had seen, certainly nothing like my own. As I stared fixedly at the moving figures, they began to have an hypnotic effect, so that when at last a hand touched my arm, I started, as if from sleep.

"It is finished", said Gurdjieff's voice, and only then I realised that the curtains had already fallen upon the stage, hiding the dancers.

I felt released; strangely aware. Yet I cried, "What does it *mean?*"

Gurdjieff smiled. "You are a ballet dancer, are you not? But perhaps, as a dancer, you do not know how to speak to your body".

I tried to tell him that dancing had always meant something special to me; that I endeavoured to express the character of the personality I was representing.

"That is not the same thing", he said impatiently. "That is for the glorification of ambition, for applause".

I was stung. "It is much more than that. It is only when I am dancing that I find myself. I believe in the disciplining of the body so that the soul is free to learn".

I stopped, embarrassed. Gurdjieff smiled again. This time he spoke more gently. "It is well. However, if you are not critical by nature, it is useless for you to remain here. But, we can talk later. Now it is time for the baths – the women first, and afterwards the men".

There seemed no end to the strange experiences of the evening. I began to feel like "Alice in Wonderland". I followed the other women into a separate building where we undressed and lay about on benches round the walls. Steam enveloped us, swirling around until I could not see across the room. Then we were hosed down with ice-cold water! When it was all over and I was dressed again, I felt invigorated, as after a Turkish bath. Later in the evening, we listened to Gurdjieff. He spoke little, but all that he said was worthwhile.

When we retired for the night, I asked Nicolas how he had got on. He chuckled. "I wish you could have seen Gurdjieff in the bath-house! He turned the steam hose on his friends until they almost screamed for mercy. He told them it was good for them!" "Well, I expect it is", I insisted, on the defensive. "He said tonight that we should become as children. What an interesting person he is, Kolia. I'm looking forward to hearing more of his ideas". Nicolas shrugged. "The bath was quite refreshing, I admit. But all the jargon seems nonsense to me".

That was not the last time I visited the Chateau du Prieure, though I never persuaded Nicolas again. I learned to know Gurdjieff well and I valued the friendship of this most unusual person. I have always liked unusual people.

CHAPTER ELEVEN

With rehearsals and practices, the days in Paris slipped away quickly, but there were many arguments regarding the new ballet "Baraban".

Though Diaghilev was not a dancer, he knew how much he could get out of people. Now he began to realise that Lifar, in spite of the considerable improvement he had made with Nicolas, would never manage the diabolical arrangement of steps which Georges Balanchine, the new choreographer, was planning for him.

"You must make them easier", Diaghilev insisted. Georges was only too anxious to please. A first-class dancer before some trouble developed in his leg, he had been appointed to his position after Diaghilev's recent disagreement with Bronislava Nijinska and was turning to good account the musical education he received in the St. Petersburg conservatoire. I could not help thinking that Diaghilev was inclined to exploit him. The new ballet Georges was creating would bring him no extra fee, but because of his disability, he would not protest.

In the evenings we used often to go to Teremok's, a café kept by a Russian who was able to serve our national meal of Stchi or suckling-pig. The pianist and even the waiters at Teremok's were Russian refugees.

I remember an evening when most of the Diaghilev company had gathered there. Georges Balanchine's wife, Gevergeva, was a singer as well as a dancer and when someone asked for a song, she walked over to the guitarists.

Danilova slipped into her place, next to Balanchine. She was a dark girl of medium height with large grey-green eyes set in a delicate face. She began to talk to Georges in low tones and I wondered if she was hoping he would keep her in mind for the new ballet. Later it transpired that she and Georges were at the beginning of a romance; I think Gevergeva must have already known that her happiness was threatened. She sang the nostalgic love songs of Russia with great feeling that night.

More and more people came in, among them young Igor, a Russian boy who had come to Paris recently and called on us, asking for lessons. The atmosphere became gayer until it was like a party. It was past midnight when we broke up at last.

Alexandra Danilova

"I am the father of the family", announced Nicolas with a lordly air. "It is for me to pay the bill". There were a few protests, but he insisted. As I have said, money meant little to him, and he was always too ready to give it away.

Walking back through the still brightly lit streets, I caught sight of a poster announcing the visit of the Indian fakir called Tara Bey.

"I'd like to go", I told Nicolas excitedly. "I've been reading about fakirs and the marvels of control they have over the body. They practise Yoga, you know".

Nicolas screwed up his face and chuckled. "I have had enough of these queer fellows. You won't get me to come with you, I'm afraid".

"Then I shall get Igor to take me", I said, knowing him already to be a little suspicious of this young man.

To my surprise, Nicolas said cheerfully: "That's right. I will speak to him myself about taking you and tell him what I shall do to him if he does not bring you home immediately after the performance".

He kept his word, and a very polite and rather subdued Igor called for me on the appointed evening.

When we arrived at the theatre in the Champs Élysées, it was quite full of people. The curtain was already up, the stage empty except for a tall vase on either side from which rose the smell of incense. From the wings came the wailing sound of an Eastern melody played on strange instruments.

As Igor and I took our seats, a deep-toned gong sounded a single note. There was a pause then Tara Bey entered. My first feeling was one of disappointment. Instead of the slim aesthetic figure I had imagined, here was a short fat man with black hair and eyes, and an enormous curly black beard.

However, he gave a magnificent performance, enduring, without a change of expression, the piercing of long sharp pins driven through his cheeks. He lay calm and still while great stones were piled on his chest and hammered into small pieces, then was put into a nailed coffin and buried under a pile of sand. He remained there for fifteen minutes and on his release bowed and smiled to his audience with a detachment which impressed me deeply. With all my heart I admired his superb control. It must surely be a triumph for the theory that the mind has power over the body.

"I wish I knew how he does it", I murmured to Igor, but I knew that it was not he who could tell me.

When the performance was over, Tara Bey threw small handfuls of Indian charms into the audience, and it suddenly seemed to me tremendously important that I should secure one, if only as a souvenir of an evening spent in awe and admiration. We were sitting in the dress circle and I turned to Igor in childlike disappointment, saying: "I'll never get one here".

I had reckoned without my young and gallant escort. Agile as a cat, he swung himself over the parapet and slid down a column at the side, to land in the centre of the auditorium. Laughing and breathless, he returned to me in triumph and dropped one of the little charms into my lap.

I was grateful, but if Igor hoped for the reward of

my interest, he was disappointed. I could think only of this man I had seen; of how one might train one's own body to such perfect control. There was so much I did not understand. One's whole life was not long enough for learning.

The day before the Diaghilev company was due to leave Paris for Brussels I heard an agitated hammering on my door. I opened it to a girl called Maroussia who had been a pupil of mine in Petrograd. We had rediscovered each other when Nicolas and I visited a small nightclub in Montmartre where her Italian husband was the manager. Now she came to tell me that Luigi had been arrested.

"What for?" I asked, drawing the girl into the room. "Truly I do not know", she said. "They came for him when I was not there. But I am sure he has done nothing wrong. Please help me".

Her appeal could not have come at a worse time. I had a rehearsal later, and there was the packing to finish. I did what I could to comfort the girl then sent her away saying Nicolas and I would try and come round to their place later that evening.

She had not been gone long when there was another knock. I gasped as I confronted Maroussia's husband.

"Luigi!" I pulled him into the room and closed the door. "What are you doing here? Maroussia has just gone. She told me". Luigi sank into a chair and put his head in his hands. "I've escaped", he said. "Can you help me to get out of France?" "But what have you done?" I asked, aghast.

It appeared that he had joined the French army in the early part of the war though he was Italian by birth. During the fighting in the South of Russia at the time of the revolution, he got separated from his regiment and crossed the border. Time elapsed and he decided not to go back. He set up a little business, met and married Maroussia and only returned to Paris when he thought it was safe. After all this time, authority had caught up with him.

It seemed stupid that he should be punished now for something that happened so long ago. I said thoughtfully, "If you could get over the frontier to Italy, they couldn't touch you there". "If", groaned Luigi. "They'll be watching for me at every station in Paris".

Already I had a plan; it was the kind of adventure that appealed to me. I ran into the bedroom and returned to dress Luigi in a full skirt and blouse, with a wide-brimmed black hat. I tied a black shawl over the hat in the fashion of the Continental flower-sellers and found a large basket in which to put Luigi's own clothes. On top of them I piled all the flowers we had. "You can buy more later". I said. "The police are not likely to recognise you now".

When Luigi had gone Nicolas came in, accompanied by Paul Dukes. They were amused at the story, and Nicolas said, "I hope he succeeds. Poor Maroussia – she must be nearly off her head with worry. We'd better go to their place after rehearsal and tell her what has happened".

It was what I hoped he would say. On our last evening in Paris, it would be nice to have an outing. Paul called for us after rehearsal and we hailed a taxi to go to Montmartre.

Arriving at the cafe, we chose a table. I could see Maroussia over in the far corner, talking to another group, but she had not seen us come in.

"Let's order champagne, Kolia", I suggested, feeling gay. "Maroussia will let us have it at half price when she knows how I got Luigi away". Nicolas made a grimace and said to Paul: "I can see this escape will cost me something!"

The band was playing a foxtrot. Nicolas did not enjoy modern dancing, but Paul looked at me. "Shall we?" he said. "Thank you". I hoped to enjoy myself, but Paul danced badly. As I sat down again, I said laughingly, "It would do you good to have some lessons in ballet". To my surprise, he took me seriously. "Do you think so? Would you teach me?" "Of course," I said. I did not really take him seriously, but remembering our conversations, I was able to tell him that I did honestly believe that control of the body helps the control of the mind, and that to be a good dancer needed discipline.

"But look", I went on. "There's Maroussia. It's time for her dance, and she still hasn't noticed us".

In the middle of her solo a man and woman came in and took their seats at a table just in front of the curtained recess through which Maroussia had made her entrance. She glanced across, faltered, and ended her dance. After a hasty bow, she ran off and disappeared behind the curtain.

"Who are those people by the door?" I asked. "Paul, do you know them?" He turned in his chair. "The man with the girl in blue? Oh, that's the Prefect of Police". I gasped. "Maroussia knew! She must have known".

Paul shrugged and smiled. "Judging by the company he's keeping, he isn't here on official business. Besides, Luigi is small fry to him". But I thought Maroussia must have had a fright of some sort. She hadn't come back for an encore. I was wondering if I ought to go to her when she came in and hurried over to our table.

"It was Luigi", she whispered breathlessly. "I saw him peeking through the curtains. He told me--" "But how foolish of him! I thought he would have been miles away by now".

"He wanted to say goodbye to me", Maroussia explained simply. "Nadia, I can't thank you enough for your help. Luigi will wear the disguise until he reaches our friends in Menton, then he'll change there and slip across the border. As soon as he gets a job he will send for me". We talked a little while longer, then Nicolas stood up. "We must go", he said. "The train leaves early tomorrow morning". In Brussels we gave a short season and left for London immediately afterwards.

PROGRAMME—*continued*

10—DIAGHILEFF RUSSIAN BALLET

Monday, December 7th
Matinee ... Aurora's Wedding
Evening ... La Boutique Fantasque

Tuesday, December 8th
Matinee ... The Good Humoured Ladies
Evening ... Cimarosiana also Prince Igor

Wednesday, December 9th
Matinee ... Petroushka
Evening ... La Boutique Fantasque

Thursday, December 10th
Matinee ... Aurora's Wedding
Evening ... Cimarosiana also Prince Igor

Friday, December 11th
Matinee ... Cimarosiana also Prince Igor
Evening ... Barabau

Saturday, December 12th
Matinee ... La Boutique Fantasque
Evening ... Cimarosiana also Prince Igor

LYDIA LOPOKOVA   STANISLAV IDZIKOVSKY
VERA NEMTCHINOVA   THADEE SLAVINSKY
LUBOV TCHERNICHEVA   NICOLAS ZVEREFF
LYDIA SOKOLOVA   SERGE LIFAR
ALICE NIKITINA   GEORGES BALANCHIN
ALEXANDRA DANILOVA   NICOLAS KREMNEFF
FELIA DOUBROVSKA   NICOLAS EFIMOFF
NADEJDA NICOLAEVA   CONSTANTIN TCHERKAS
TAMARA GEVERGEVA   JEAN JAZVINSKY
VERA SAVINA   MICHAEL FEDOROFF
LEON WOIZIKOVSKY   MICHAEL PAVLOV
MAESTRO NICOLAS LEGAT
And Corps de Ballet

Stage Director - - - - M. SERGE GRIGORIEFF
Conductor - - - - ROGER DESORMIÈRE
Leader - - - - WYNNE REEVES

In London again we had a pleasant reunion at the house in Golders Green. Everyone was cheerful and the tiny nag of worry, which had haunted me since receiving my father's letter in Rome, was at last dissipated.

The Diaghilev ballet appeared nightly at the London Coliseum, Nicolas taking the parts which Cecchetti had previously performed. In "La Boutique Fantasque" he was the shopkeeper, with Serge Lifar as his young assistant, in "Petroushka" he was the Showman, and in "Carnaval", Pantalon.

Diaghilev never did things by halves and having secured the services of the one-time leading dancer of Russia, he meant to use him to the full.

To take all these roles and be ballet-master as well was something of a strain for Nicolas. At the studio, we were busy, too, for dancers who had heard that we were back now wanted lessons. The greater part of this work fell on me. I arranged, too, for a satisfactory handing-over when we should leave London again to go on tour.

The obvious fact that Nan had not been practising her dancing as she should did not greatly disturb me. As the doctor had pointed out, she was growing fast, and I remembered he had advised us not to press her against her will.

We left London again early in December; our destination Berlin. Some of the company went by the Hook of Holland (the cheapest route) but Diaghilev insisted that Nicolas and I must join him and Lifar in their special carriage travelling via Calais and Paris.

I wondered if this would not cause more jealousy, but Nicolas assured me it was necessary as Diaghilev wanted to discuss with him the forthcoming productions. Certainly, arguments went on between them throughout the whole journey, Diaghilev declaring his intention to give only modern ballets in Berlin, Nicolas trying to persuade him against it.

Afterwards, when we were alone, Nicolas told me wryly, "I might as well have saved my breath, for of course he will have his way. In any case, I shall see he doesn't include you in these modern creations. They would not suit you, and I know you hate them as much as I do!"

I felt I must support his views and did not point out that it was torture to me to be a member of a company, yet not to dance. I hoped that Diaghilev would change his mind.

It was almost Christmas. In Berlin, Nicolas and I stayed at a pension with some of the unattached boys of the Company with whom we were friendly. We found them less biased and petty than the ballerinas, and they revered Nicolas as Maestro. They were also very nice to me, carrying my shopping or waiting on me after we returned from the theatre. Nicolas said laughingly that we reminded him of Snow White and her attendant dwarfs.

"Except that in this case it is I who am the dwarf!"

I said ruefully. "I always wanted to be taller".

We had our own little Christmas tree at the pension and the boys collected money for presents to hang upon it. On Christmas Eve, the Russian festival, we gave a party for any of the company who liked to come, as well as to some of the Russian refugees who were now to be found in any city on the Continent. Among these was old Constantine Savich, onetime President of the St. Petersburg Court and a friend of my parents. He used to give talks in Berlin and Paris, refuting the claims of the woman who said she was the surviving daughter of the murdered Tsar. It is doubtful whether anyone will ever know the truth, but Savich was obsessed by the subject and later collaborated with Pierre Gilliari (a former tutor to the Princess) to produce a book called "La Fausse Anastasie".

It was a good party. Towards midnight, we all gathered like children around the Christmas tree to receive our little gifts. When the lights were turned low, and the candles lit, a somber quiet descended upon us, for many of us were thinking of Russia, of our lost homes, of the fact that we could never go back...

Feeling an almost intolerable nostalgia come over me, I jumped up and switched on the lights. Dwelling on such things was not profitable.

"Put on the gramophone, boys", I cried. "And bring in the cruchon".

They carried in the huge jar of liquor – a kind of cocktail – and everyone lifted their glasses and drank to each other. In the height of the merrymaking, Serge Lifar walked in, alone.

I ran over to welcome him, talking rather loudly in the hope that he would not hear the teasing comments of the other boys. It was not often, certainly, that Lifar could escape. Presently the party began to get a little out of hand. A man who was separated from his wife retired behind the piano to weep and repeat his beloved's name, and some of the boys, egged on by the girls, sprayed him with soda water. Voices became too loud, dancing too wild. I escaped to my room for a brief respite and found Nicolas there, playing poker with some of the older guests.

"Join us", he said, turning to smile a welcome as I entered. I shook my head. "No thank you Kolia. After this party, I am broke". "I will lend you some money".

But I declined. When gambling one must at least play with one's own money. Otherwise, it is bad luck. I sat down a little wearily on a chair and taking up a ballet shoe, pretended to be darning it. It was silly, perhaps, to feel sad on Christmas Eve, to long so overwhelmingly for what was past. I thought of Gurdjieff's words, "In the river of life, suffering is not intentional. In conscious life, suffering is intentional and of great value…"

"How are our visitors getting on?" Nicolas asked.

The bad moment was over. I was able to look up and smile.

"They are enjoying themselves, I suppose. But, what

do you think? Should we break it up soon? There's a rehearsal tomorrow morning, and we shall none of us be much good". "A rehearsal on Christmas Day?" exclaimed a friend.

Nicolas left his game quite soon and we went into the room together. Now the place was a shambles, and our guests in still more riotous mood. We had to exercise tact in persuading them to go. As we all said goodnight, I noticed the Japanese professor, Mitamori, watching our embraces with disapproval.

"Do you not say goodbye like this in Japan?" I asked him smiling. He looked shocked. "Indeed no." "Then how? Supposing you were leaving a party and saying goodbye to your hostess?" Professor Mitamori put his palms together and with a grave expression bowed low from the waist. "I do not approve. Mitamori, I shall go to Japan and convert them. It will be fun showing them just how nice it is to kiss".

Christmas came and went, but in January, there were poorly filled houses to greet the performances at the theatre. The season of modern ballets was not proving successful. Secretly, Nicolas was triumphant.

"Did I not tell you so?" he said to me. "The Germans are sentimental people. They don't understand these new ideas, and they don't want to".

Presently it was rumoured that the season was to be shortened, and Diaghilev went off to raise more money. When he returned, he advertised that the company would give for their final performances, "Prince

Igor", "Lac des Cygnes", "La Boutique Fantasque", and "Scheherazade". Immediately the booking office reported increased sales, and it was decided to continue for another two weeks after all.

CHAPTER TWELVE

At the end of January, we travelled to the south of France. Without the Monte Carlo contract, it is doubtful whether the Diaghilev Company could have carried on its existence. Though the actual season of performances covered only about two weeks in the spring and another two in the winter, the support from the Casino management and the patronage of the Princess of Monaco did much for prestige as well as finances. The company usually remained in Monte Carlo for some time; dancing in the operas and at important parties, preparing the new ballets and polishing up the rest of their repertoire.

It was a good time for the artists. To Nicolas, as well as to me, it was like another holiday. Everyone wanted to know us, and we were constantly invited to parties or for drives along the corniches to see glorious views of the Riviera coastline.

One very hot day, soon after our arrival, Nicolas and I sat on the terrace of the Café de Paris, sipping an aperitif and watching the crowds pour into the Casino. I remember that I wore a green dress with a large Leghorn hat. Nicolas kept taking off his own grey felt and mopping his brow. "Leave it off", I said. "You are getting nicely sunburned".

It suited him. I thought how young he looked, in spite of his almost-bald head, his figure as trim and his blue eyes alert and lively as a child's.

"I cannot imagine", he said now, "how people can

bear to be shut up in the Casino on such a lovely day. They surely cannot enjoy the stuffy atmosphere and the grabbing. Even the winners stay too long and inevitably lose again". "Are you sure you wouldn't feel differently if you were able to gamble?" I asked him teasingly.

No artist employed by the Casino was allowed to play the tables, and I was told that the taboo originated with Chaliapin. It appears that, some years before, when the singer was in Monte Carlo for an Opera season, he went to the Casino day after day and eventually gambled away the whole of his salary, at which he made a great fuss, saying it could not be right for his earnings to go back to the same management that paid him. It was agreed at last to refund his losses; the new rule being made to ensure that such a thing could not happen again.

As we sat on, lazy and contented in the warm sunshine, Nicolas suddenly exclaimed: "Why there's Paul! He didn't say he was coming here. Let us go and talk to him". I glanced at my watch. "I must not stop. I'm due at the theatre for a rehearsal". "I'll follow you", Nicholas said. "I will have a word with Paul first".

Arriving at the rehearsal room, I was greeted with the news that Karsavina was coming out to join the company. A few days earlier Vera Nemchinova had caused some consternation by going off to join her friend, Nicolas Zverev, in Massine's little revue company. Her defection angered Diaghilev who liked dismissal to be on his side, it also put him into a difficulty regarding the new "Romeo and Juliet". Now Karsavina was to partner Lifar in this.

"Do you know her?" someone asked me. "But of course. She was in Nicolas's class at the Maryinsky and he knew her father well".

Serge Lifar came up and drew me aside. "Diaghilev wants us to dance together in Les Biches", he told me in a low tone. "But don't say anything yet".

I was pleased at the idea. The choreography of Les Biches was by Bronislava Nijinska. Now back with us again after her previous disagreement with Diaghilev. Always trying to advance my technique, La Nijinska's tours de force dancing roles appealed to me, and I looked forward to this one. As soon as there was an opportunity, I told Nicolas about it and he rejoiced with me.

"That's good. You will enjoy that", he said. He threw me an amused glance. "I've something to tell you, too. We are going to have another pupil".

In Monte Carlo we had been approached by several people wanting lessons. The money was useful to send home, besides giving us another interest. There was something in Nicolas's tone, however, that told me this was no ordinary young ballet student.

"Tell me who it is", I demanded. Nicolas laughed. "You'd never guess! It's Paul. I understand you told him it would do him good to have ballet lessons and that you would teach him. He has decided to take you at your word". "I only said it in fun", I protested. "It was that evening we went to Luigi's when we danced together. His feet were so stiff, and he kept treading on me". "Well, you know he developed frostbite in his toes some years ago when he was doing intelligence work in Russia. I've been talking to him, and it is quite possible ballet might do him good".

I suddenly had an idea. "Kolia, if I could find somewhere to give lessons, we could take more pupils". Nicolas wondered if it was worth it. We should not be in Monte Carlo long, he argued. I talked him round to my point of view and set off at once to try to find suitable premises. An agent put me in touch with a teacher of ballroom dancing who agreed to let me hire his hall for a few hours every day.

When I returned to our hotel, the clerk at the desk informed me a gentleman was waiting for me in the vestibule. I walked across to the man he indicated and with a start of surprise recognised my brother-in-law.

"Andrey! How nice to see you. So, you got Kolia's letter?"

I held out my hand, trying to hide my distress. Nicolas had not seen his sister and her husband for years, but knowing they now lived in Monaco he wrote telling them of our visit and where they would be able to get in touch with us. I could scarcely believe that this shabby man could be Count Andrey Chouvalov.

When Nicolas' sister Vera married Andrey, he was a brilliant general in charge of the Tsar's own bodyguard.

The couple moved in the highest Russian society and were friends of Madame Kshesinskaya. We had heard that Andrey led a company of wild Cossacks against the Tsar's enemies during the revolution and later that he had, like ourselves, lost all he possessed. I was, however, unprepared for such a violent change. Now he wore a soiled trench coat, a battered hat much too large for him, and old shoes that gaped at the soles and were tied with string. He smiled at me nervously.

"Vera wouldn't come. She said she couldn't look smart enough". "What nonsense! As if that mattered, but I'm very glad you came, Andrey. You must have lunch with us. Come up to our room and we'll have a chat until Kolia comes in."

Andrey drew back. "I came only to apologise for both of us. I can't have lunch with you, looking like this". He glanced down at himself with a deprecating air. "They are the only clothes I have. As for these shoes…"

"I'm still proud of you", I told him warmly. I hesitated, not wishing to offend him. "Let me buy you a pair of shoes. We could go to the shop and get them now".

He demurred a little, then gave in. As we went along the street, however, he suddenly turned to me.

"If you are really willing to waste money on us, I would prefer to spend it on some perfume for Vera. It is one of the things she misses most".

"But Andrey – you need shoes". "Vera needs perfume", he declared obstinately.

He was so insistent that I had to let him do as he wished. When we returned to the hotel he was carrying the box containing a bottle of Rose Jacomineau, the perfume which was his wife's favourite. While Andrey greeted Nicolas, I had to turn my head away to hide my tears. Vera had been a great beauty and as the wife of one of the wealthiest men in Russia, lived in luxury. Now a bottle of perfume was but a reminder of the past...

"You must see Vera, Kolia", I told Nicolas when Andrey had gone. "We might be able to do something for them. I have found my hall, and we shall be able to take more pupils".

Nicolas shook his head at me. "As if you had not already enough people to help".

Madame Nijinska did not look like the usual type of dancer, she had the same strong legs that had made her brother's elevation phenomenal, also, the same slanting eyes and high cheekbones. Bronia's character was forceful, and she could be bullied by no one, not even Diaghilev.

On arriving at Monte Carlo, she refused to take his word that Lifar had improved beyond his hopes. Serge had been her pupil when she had her own school in Kiev, and perhaps she wished people to remember this. She watched him carefully as he took a private lesson with Nicolas, from whom she herself had learned at the Imperial School.

"You have done wonders with him, Maestro", she agreed at last. "He works hard", said Nicolas. He laughed and glanced slyly at Lifar. "I heard a rumour that he even goes down to the jetty at night to practise jumps. Is that true, Serge?" Lifar smiled and shrugged his shoulders. He was used to the gossip that surrounded him and he had learned to keep his own counsel.

When we asked Madame Nijinska for the latest news of her brother Vaslav, she shook her head. "There is no change", she said sadly. "He continues to live in a world of his own, and it is difficult to rouse him for anything".

In Monte Carlo, the company met for classes each morning at nine. These continued until about half-past ten when we had a break for coffee and then a rehearsal followed. Constant Lambert was the pianist; a thin, impatient person who, except when playing the piano, could not be still but paced up and down nervously. He had composed the music for the new ballet "Romeo and Juliet" which had already run into difficulties.

Diaghilev was a late riser, and it was usually after eleven when he joined us. His presence was terrifying to some. Broodily slumped in his chair, his gaze fixed on the dancers, he interrupted with advice and suggestions or to make one of the younger members repeat a single gesture five or six times before pronouncing himself satisfied. If a previous performance had been below standard, he did not hesitate to include the whole company in devastating censure. During the time we were at Monte Carlo he was more than usually hard to please and in spite of the recent holiday, he did not look well. It was understood that his diabetes was plaguing him acutely.

To my great disappointment, I learned now that I was not to partner Serge Lifar in Les Biches after all. Nicolas was indignant and, in spite of my protest, insisted on tackling Diaghilev and reminding him of his promises.

Diaghilev merely shrugged and explained curtly that another ballerina had pestered him for the role. "There were financial obligations involved and I knew Nadia wouldn't make a silly fuss", he finished.

Certainly, it was not my wish to make a fuss. I knew that the company was always on the verge of financial crisis and I knew, too, just what the obligations were. But the explanation did not altogether satisfy me.

I wondered if Serge had foolishly revealed his premature disclosure to me. Perhaps Nicolas's independent manner had offended the great man. Or had Diaghilev perhaps seen that very unflattering cartoon Nicolas drew last week? In Russia, Nicolas had been a law unto himself, and now he did not feel, as many did, any particular reverence for Diaghilev or his pronouncements. There was nothing I could do about it. Rehearsals, performances, and teaching took up most of my time, and I pushed the disturbing thoughts away.

The Duke of Connaught and some of his friends were coming to watch the final rehearsal of the ballets. A row of gilt chairs awaited the distinguished guests and Diaghilev stalked up and down, supervising the drinks and seeing that everything was in order. I thought he seemed in a nervous mood.

At almost the last minute before the arrival of his patron he came over to Nicolas where he stood, talking to me. He was frowning and did not lower his voice, "We shall be giving 'Carnaval' first, as you know. I hope you will dance Pantalon in your most pleasing manner. Nothing to give offence. For pity's sake don't make him such a pansy".

Nicolas was slow to anger, but proud. His chin lifted. "I have been dancing Pantalon for many years", he said stiffly. "I cannot interpret the role in anything but my own way. As yet it has never given offence".

Diaghilev glared, but Nicolas turned away with a shrug and I knew he was not intimidated. He danced the role brilliantly, as he had always done, convulsing his audience with laughter and drawing loud applause. When I glanced across at Diaghilev, I saw that his face still wore a brooding look, and I felt we had not heard the last of the matter.

I had been given little to do, only appearing in a brief pas de trois. There were a few other divertissements and the performance ended with Lifar's version of "L'apres midi d'un Faune"; the dance that Diaghilev had always wanted for him, but which only reminded most people that Nijinsky's brilliance could not be recreated.

Afterwards, some of the dancers were entertained by the distinguished guests, and a small stout man asked me to go for a drive in his car. Boris Kochno, overhearing my refusal, afterwards expressed surprise. You should have gone with him, Nadia. Don't you know, he is a wealthy oil king from South America?" "Indeed" I said laughing. "But then, I do not need oil".

During the next few days, I could not shake off the feeling that Nicolas and Diaghilev were near to a quarrel. There was not much chance to brood over it, however, for my spare time was fully occupied with teaching. Paul Dukes, to my surprise, proved an unusually apt pupil, and I told him it was a pity he had not taken up dancing before.

Paul Dukes

"You would have been good", I said. He laughed. "*Would* have been? There is time yet".

The whole company was invited to a party one day, at a house on Cap Martin. Wandering round the extensive grounds with Nicolas I felt a renewal of my nostalgia. Artists of our standing in Russia had once had homes like this; now we were forced to lead a Nomadic existence having no real foundation.

But what – I reminded myself – was the use of a philosophy if one did not put it to the acid test? Gurdjieff had pronounced, "The worse the conditions of life, the greater the possibility of productive work". I must try to believe that.

Hotel life in Monte Carlo was expensive. Discovering that Georges Balanchine was having financial difficulties like ourselves, Nicolas and I combined forces with him and his friend, Dmitri, and rented a small villa. Soon afterwards, Georges came to me with a new suggestion. He had learned that the Hotel Metropole required entertainers and he suggested that he and I might practise a pas de deux and apply.

I could have said quite truly that I already had enough to do, but I knew Georges needed the extra money and I fell in with the suggestion. We had scarcely begun rehearsals of our act, however, when Diaghilev's spies brought the matter to his ears. He sent for me and said brusquely:

"According to your agreement with me you cannot do this, Nicolaeva". I stared at him in amazement for he, himself, had arranged for me to dance with Idzikowsky at several outside functions. "Georges needs the money", I pointed out. "His salary is insufficient for all he has to do now". Diaghilev shrugged. "He is only young, and he is not worth any more. You must tell him to give up this idea".

I could do nothing else. Though in many ways I liked Diaghilev and admired his immense capabilities.

I deplored his ruthless attitude to those in his employ. I knew that Nicolas would not submit to too much direction, and already I saw the beginning of the end.

One small disagreement followed another. Matters came to a head when Nicolas refused to appear in the last scene of "Pantalon", saying it was beneath his dignity to caper round the small stage in the Farandole, hand-in-hand with Markova.

"I will not make myself so ridiculous!" he fumed, and nothing could move him.

He and Diaghilev quarreled bitterly, and Nicolas resigned his position. Diaghilev was full of self-righteous indignation. He always termed any defection "disloyalty", regardless of the fact that he, himself, had made the position untenable.

Now he told me that I, at least, must remain with the company. I could guess the reason for this; on Nemchinova's departure, I had immediately taken over her role in "Petroushka" and there was no one to replace me.

"If Nicolas is to leave the company, I must leave too", I said obstinately. But when Diaghilev pointed out that I was still under contract to him, I had to submit. But not for long – I told myself – not for long…

In May, the company left Monte Carlo for Paris, where we were to have a season at the Sarah Bernhardt theatre. Nicolas came with me, of course, but I had become more than ever anxious to get out of my contract as soon as possible. Grigoriev and his wife, Tchernichova—now teaching—seemed determined to slight me, and when Ninette de Valois came from London to rejoin the company she was given the part which had hitherto been mine; one of the two leads in "Sylphides". I vowed I would not dance in "Petroushka" as billed, even though Diaghilev himself had praised my performance and said I was his best in this role.

"You will have to dance it", I told Danilova. "My knee is troubling me, and I shall go to the doctor about it". "I will not dance in 'Petroushka' at such short notice", Danilova declared. "There is not time to learn it properly".

When I produced a doctor's certificate to say I was not to dance, however, it was obvious that something would have to be done. A telegram was dispatched to Lydia Lopokova, summoning her to take over from me. Diaghilev was angry and now did not care if I left. When the company left Paris, I knew I should not be with them. Nicolas and I could make other plans.

Nicolaeva

CHAPTER THIRTEEN

In Paris now was a woman called Djina Saari. Lancashire-born, she had spent much of her life in the East and had financed and promoted various small companies. Now she was behind the idea of a permanent ballet-company at the Theatre des Champs Élysées. She knew Nicolas by reputation and approached him, suggesting that he should produce the ballets and that I should be the Prima Ballerina.

We agreed and began at once to work with her.

Djina Saari was fair, plump and good-looking; a dynamic personality. In the mornings, she stayed in bed, making arrangements over the phone, or she would summon Nicolas to discuss various problems. At last, she got up and dressed, taking endless trouble over her appearance. After which, with a drink at her side and a chain-sequence of cigarettes, she could work until late at night.

One of the first problems was to find a new partner for me. It grieved Nicolas to admit it, but his arm could no longer stand the strain of even my light weight.

We had recently met Anatole Oboukhoff again – the young relative with whom we worked in Russia. He had been partnering a dancer called Elena Smirnova, now awaiting an operation on her knee. Nicolas said now, "You and Anatole always danced well together, Nadia. Why not ask Elena if she is willing?"

It is recognised in the ballet world that a male dancer who has been partnering a ballerina exclusively for some time becomes almost like her own property. She can dispose of him if she wishes or lend him temporarily to someone else; always the ballerina is the operating half of the partnership.

Oboukhoff was somewhat nervous about the outcome of my interview with Elena and refused to be present. But his partner consented willingly to the transfer, saying it had worried her that Anatole would have to suffer monetarily through her disablement. When I returned with the good news Anatole was so relieved that he swung me off the ground, and lifting me high above his head, swung me round at a furious pace. Nicolas hovered below in anxiety, saying: "Careful, Anatole, careful".

It was a long time since I had felt such exhilaration, such happy abandon. I pressed my arms to my sides, my hands turned outwards like the fins of a fish, my back hollowed so that my body formed a crescent. Oboukhoff tossed me into the air and I turned a somersault to land neatly in his arms as he knelt on one knee to receive me. We smiled triumphantly at Nicolas who was mopping his forehead in relief. "I don't mind you risking your own life, Anatole", he said crossly, "but I will not have you risking Nadia's". "It isn't as dangerous as it looks", I assured him. "Don't you remember that Anatole and I did 'the fish' before?"

I reminded him also of a ballet which I had danced in Russia not long before we left. "The Laugh of the Red Mask" was taken from a story by Edgar Allen Poe and arranged by Galizovsky. Though the committee later turned it down, pronouncing it sensational and inartistic, I enjoyed the acrobatic adventure. Now my recent encounters with Ouspensky and Gurdjieff explained that enjoyment; discipline of the body, they preached, was a prelude to the release of the mind, and I proved this to be true.

Later that evening Nicolas remarked, as he had done so many times before, that he was too old for me; that I should have married a younger man. I knew he was sad that he could no longer partner me, even though he had long ago faced the fact that this time must come and had spoken of it.

"You are still my *Masetro*", I told him. "There will never be a time when I cannot learn from you".

The love of my life was stage work, however, and I wanted to go on. In any case, there were financial commitments in which I was heavily involved. My father had been ill again, and it was my treasured ambition to get him and my mother to France,

Self-Caricature 1931

Nan too, for reports concerning her health continued to disquiet us.

So, my partnership with Oboukhoff continued. Nicolas created a new ballet called "Vengeance des Dieux", taken from a Hindu legend. Critics spoke of my technique as "masterly" and said that my pas de deux with Oboukhoff would "grace" the stage of the Opera.

Apart from our regular appearances in the theatre my partner and I sought outside engagements at parties and nightclubs, and with the extra money earned I was able to rent a little villa in Fontainebleu and bring the family over. As soon as I saw Nan again and talked with my mother, I was convinced that other advice should be taken. I consulted a Russian specialist who examined Nan and after studying her x-rays advised me to take her to Professor Calot of the Institute Calot at Berck-Plage, Boulogne. The Professor diagnosed tuberculosis of the spine and said that Nan must be admitted to the Institute where she would probably be on her back for at least two years!

My own distress was, of course, nothing compared with Nan's when she learned that she must be cut off from all that a girl of her age should be able to enjoy. No philosophy or reasoning could convince her that life was not utterly a tragedy.

The trouble was traced, of course, to the fall she had while trying to emulate the antics of the Hoffman girls; a small crack in the spine proved a breeding-ground for the disease. For my part, it was of no use to indulge in regrets. The treatment at the Institute was an additional expense which work must pay for. I could only pray that Professor Calot would eventually be successful in curing Nan.

She was not a patient invalid. Reports of misbehaviour and rebellion

Nan at Berck-Plage

came constantly from the authorities and again I did not know just how to help. We sent to England for Miss Ward, hoping that in the continuation of her studies Nan would find a new interest. But all too soon staunch Miss Ward had to return to England owing to family troubles and after that there was a long procession of English and French governesses, none of them staying long. Poor Nan! It certainly seemed that she had been given too many trials in her short life.

Meanwhile we had our own trials. Though the Djina Saari Company played to full houses, productions always seemed to cost more money than was expected, and it proved a losing battle for a woman whose capital was limited.

One evening, during a performance, news was whispered back-stage. "Have you heard? Diaghilev is in the audience!"

Many dancers hoped he might have come to select new recruits for his company and were excited at the prospect. Nicolas and I, alone, were undisturbed. We felt that Diaghilev's visit could make no difference to us. But in this we were wrong, for some few days later three members of the company received invitations to throw in their lot with Diaghilev. Among these three was my own partner – Oboukhoff!

He came to me in agitation, saying that he did not want to let me down, but I must surely see that it was a wonderful chance. I had no alternative but to release him; a dissatisfied partner is worse than useless, in any case. Apart from my own loss, the removal of three of our best dancers left the little company devitalized and precipitated its break-up.

What with one thing and another it seemed that

our luck had run out. Nicolas was dispirited, but when friends suggested that he ought to open a studio in Paris, he revived. In training dancers, he was expert and could not be dictated to. "What about you?" he asked.

"You must know that my only wish is to dance", I told him. "And it is obvious that a studio cannot support us all". Through the efforts of my brother, a house was offered in the Rue des Petits Ecuries. Vladimir thought it would do, but I was not sure. My brother argued that the premises were in the right district for a ballet school, while I pointed out that now shops and factories were springing up all round it was not as desirable. The conversion would cost a great deal; more than we could afford at this time.

However, I found that Vladimir had already persuaded Nicolas into acceptance so there was no point in being pessimistic. I was proved right on one point. The conversion absorbed almost the whole of our small capital, and it was more than ever necessary for me to begin earning as soon as possible.

I discovered a young Pole called Smarslik (he later became Stanley Barry) and after some private practice presented him to Nicolas for his approval. For half an hour the young man was put through his paces. He was good-looking and strong and could lift me with an easy grace.

"I think he will be all right", said Nicolas, "when he has had a bit more practice".

The new studio was called "Haute-Ecole de Ballet", and soon became known to some of the greatest dancers from all over the world. Whenever they were in Paris, they went to Nicolas for lessons, listening as attentively as any novice to his suggestions for improvement.

To the studio came girls from the Opera who were not so concerned about the advancement of their technique; they wanted only to learn how to do the more spectacular steps; fouettes, pirouettes and manege and these as quickly as possible.

Smarslik and I had already been booked for a tour of Holland and Sweden. We practised at the new Studio and one day I asked Nicolas if he had noticed that Smarslik seemed attracted to a girl from the Opera, a Danish girl called Gertrude.

Nicolas made a comical grimace. "She is certainly attractive, but it takes a woman to scent romance. I do not suppose there is anything serious between Gertrude and Smaralik".

I hoped he was right, but I was almost sure that the couple were in love. Apart from any effect it might have on our partnership, they would naturally try to hide it for the girl came of a good family and was brought to us by an aunt who was keeping an eye on her. I did not grudge Smarslik and Gertrude a romance if it brought them happiness, but I felt it would be disastrous if my partner should request a release now.

A week later my suppositions were proved correct.

Smarslik did not wait to ask for his release. He and Gertrude eloped secretly, and the aunt actually came to me and accused me of connivance in the affair!

The total waste of my work with Smarslik was not the only trouble. I knew I could not afford to cancel the Dutch tour. When Nicolas suggested that a comparatively new pupil of his should ultimately be trained to take Smarslik's place, I was impatient to begin at once.

Jean Mercier was a young man whose father had been killed in the war. As a ward of the nation the French Government had made themselves responsible for a training in whatever career he might choose. He chose ballet, and after attending a school for some years was coming to Nicolas for advanced lessons.

He was delighted with the idea of becoming my partner and we began to rehearse assiduously. I found him easy to work with; strong and intuitive. In a very short time, I was announcing to Nicolas my intention of fulfilling the engagement I had not cancelled in Holland.

"I believe it would be better if Jean had a Russian name to match mine", I finished. "What do you think of 'Serge Renoff'?" "One name is as good as another to kill yourself with, I suppose", Nicolas said gloomily, "which is what you will do if you take him on yet".

"Please, Kolia – you have not seen us lately. Let us show you what we can do", I begged. I knew that Nicolas was not impressed with our exhibition, but I talked him round. A couple of weeks later 'Renoff' and I departed for Holland.

After our first performance, the manager of the theatre asked to speak to me on my own. "Why are you using this boy?" he said. "He is not good enough for you. It would be better if you danced alone". "He will improve", I insisted. I had faith in Renoff and wanted to continue the partnership. For a while, I increased the number of my own solos and kept the pas de deux

Serge Renoff

to a character dance, at the same time continuing our practice. Afterwards Renoff and I danced in Copenhagen, Germany, Alexandria, and Algiers with great success.

By the time we reached this last destination, I was somewhat exhausted with all the travelling. The heat in Algiers made it impossible to sleep and all night long, I would toss restlessly in bed, to rise in the morning unrefreshed. The longing for sleep became an obsession, so that when I passed the coffee taverns and saw men with their heads lolling comfortably on their chests, I regarded them with envy.

"I wish I could sleep like that", I told Renoff. "They look completely relaxed".

Renoff laughed and pointed out the long pipes lying slackly in the men's hands. "They have been smoking hashish. This is what makes them sleep".

I did not say any more to him, but later I fingered some similar pipes in a shop and asked the salesman if he thought I could learn to smoke hashish.

He looked shocked and shook his head vigorously. "Madame – it would make you sick", he said.

I suppose I looked disappointed for he called after me as I turned away, saying that he could sell me some cigarettes with only a little hashish in them.

Tarantella with Renoff

I bought some and going back to my hotel room lay on the bed, smoking one of the cigarettes. At first, it had a soothing effect, and I closed my eyes, deliciously sure that I would have a long refreshing sleep at last. Suddenly the room seemed to be swinging around me and my body felt so light that it appeared to be floating away. I sat up, terrified, and with my last ounce of strength called out for someone to help me.

Renoff heard, and came running along the passage to stand in the doorway and exclaim: "Nadia – what is it?" I held my head in my hands and sobbed wildly:

"I'm going up! Hold me down, oh, hold me down!" It was some time before this dreadful feeling wore off. Then I lay back, pale and shaken. "The first time of smoking hashish will also be my last", I affirmed in disgust. "I thought it would just make me sleep…"

Soon after this, Renoff and I went back to Paris for an engagement at the Apollo theatre. Nicolas was established now in the Paris studio, and had many pupils, among whom was Paul Dukes, who still persevered with his dancing.

My mother and father were happy at Fontainebleu, and a visit to Berck-Plage confirmed Professor Calot's reports that Nan's disease was yielding to treatment. I was enjoying the renewal of family ties when a producer who had seen Renoff and me dancing at the Apollo, invited us to take part in a new show called "Allelulia" which was to be put on in Barcelona. Bills must be paid, and I had no choice but to accept.

Arriving at the theatre dressing room in Barcelona, on the day of the first performance, I was presented with a beautiful white net gown which had just arrived from Paris. It had been made to my measurements, but the skirt consisted entirely of rows of tiny frills and was lined with half-a-dozen stiffened petticoats. In spite of its beauty, I gazed at it in horror. It would fill most of the stage, and my partner would not be able to get within inches of me.

There was no time for alterations. I asked for a pair of scissors and with impatient haste began to snip away the underskirts. My dresser hovered round me in agitation. "No, Madame– please – you must not !"When I went on snipping she rushed away to find the Manager who came to implore in his turn, "Please, Madame – do not cut this lovely dress for which I have paid five thousand pesetas!" I suspended the scissors for a moment, demanding: "How can I dance with a partner, bunched up in all this?" "It need be only for tonight", he pleaded. "Then I will take the dress for another number and have made for you something simpler". With that, I was forced to agree, but neither Renoff nor I forgot the agonised restriction of that first performance.

"Allelulia" ran for almost a year. For the first part of the time, I stayed in a Barcelona hotel, but later I became a paying guest with a private family. It was cheaper and besides I liked local life and wanted to learn the language. The change was a happy one. The simple kindly family made me welcome, laughed at my mistakes, and put me right. Food was good and plentiful, the whole family sitting round a big table for meals. Above the table swung a bottle, suspended from the ceiling by a rope. It had two divisions, one for wine and the other for water. Each person in turn removed the cork from the side from which they wished to drink, tilting the bottle so that the liquid poured in a thin stream into the mouth. It became a joke to watch my unsuccessful efforts and they roared with laughter when water ran down my neck. "It is as well I do not drink wine", I would admit ruefully. "I shall never be able to do it properly".

It was in the latter part of our stay in Barcelona that Madame Nijinska saw us dance. She had left Diaghilev and was now ballet-mistress for Ida Rubenstein's company. She suggested that Renoff and I should join them for the season in Paris. I jumped at the chance. Paris was home for me now.

CHAPTER FOURTEEN

Ida Rubenstein was tall and striking. A pupil of Michael Fokine, she was Diaghilev's first "Cleopatra", a role which suited her, for it was almost all mime. Later Diaghilev criticised her cruelly, but this might have been because he envied her wealth and wished that the money she was able to spend on her lavish productions had come, instead, to him.

With gorgeous costumes and splendid décor by Bakst and Benois, some of Diaghilev's own most accomplished dancers and a ballet-mistress like La Nijinska, how was it possible for the Ida Rubenstein ballets to be dismissed so contemptuously? Certainly, the performances were always sold out and gave pleasure to many.

But it is true that the members of her company were sometimes amused by Madame Rubenstein. She had many strange mannerisms and was not self-critical. In the ballet "Le Baiser de la Fee" which now we began immediately to rehearse, she elected to be Psyche, with Anatole Viltzak as her Cupid. Anatole was a fine dancer, trained at the Maryinsky, but he was a little short; when he was supposed to be hunting Psyche between archways of flowers, he was sometimes hidden while Ida still remained magnificently visible. Some of the boys in the corps de ballet made much of this, and would chant wickedly under their breath: "Goodbye forever, she'll catch him, never…"

Owing to the unusual number of rehearsals, the

company also spoke of them as of "Les Ballets de Repetition de Madame Ida Rubenstein". But these are only the sort of jokes usually made at the expense of those in authority.

We appeared for the first time at the Paris Opera House on November the twenty-second, 1928. When Ida annexed Renoff as her partner, I danced with Serge Unger, one of the boys who joined Diaghilev's company at the same time as Lifar. I was also a soloist in six of the ballets, and Andre Levinson, the distinguished critic, referred to "Mademoiselle Nicolaeva, au métier de virtuoso".

Diaghilev, himself, came to one of our performances when he was in Paris. Perhaps his scathing remarks about the production in general were prompted by professional jealousy, but later, in a letter to Lifar, he mentioned my pas de deux with Unger as something "worth seeing". For that alone, he declared, he was not sorry to be present.

Apart from my performances, however, I was glad to be back in Paris. From there I could go and see my mother and father, and also visit Nan. My father was very frail now, but we were still able to have our long talks and he was always eager to hear what new views I had conceived about the 'unknown'. Sometimes Paul came with me to Fontainbleu and we all argued together.

Paul had improved his dancing immensely since his lessons with Nicolas and now he, Renoff, and I began to train under a tough little Frenchman by the name of Saulnier, who had a gymnasium in Montmartre. Renoff went in for acrobatics just for the fun of it, but Paul and I, both vegetarians and yogi-enthusiasts, enjoyed this kind of dancing for the special states of consciousness the physical tests invoked.

Whenever I could spare the time, I dashed over to see Nan at Berck-Plage. She was allowed out of the institute for short periods now and wore a sort of steel corset that irked her greatly. I sometimes took her to the nearby beach, where she stared resentfully at girls who were more fortunate; girls who could run lightly across the sands with their boyfriends and plunge happily into the sea.

My lessons with Nicolas began again and continued daily all the time I was in Paris. His studio was still the rendezvous of first-class dancers; the better they were, the more anxious to keep their technique at peak. From the regular company of the Opera came girls who, as before, were content with showy steps which looked more difficult than they were, and there was the usual sprinkling of amateurs.

In my absence I found that August Albo, the Estonian sculptor, had executed in bronze a very fine head of Nicolas. I have it now in the entrance hall of my dancing school in Kent. It is a striking likeness.

The Paris season at the Opera ended on December the fourth, and in January, we gave five performances in Monte Carlo, which were spoken of in the papers as a "succéss triumphal"; the last performance opening in an atmosphere of tremendous enthusiasm. My dancing in "Nocturne" earned glowing applause.

August Albo and Nicolas Legat

We continued in the company throughout its tour of Central Europe: Italy, Spain, Belgium and Holland. Then I began to feel it might be better for Renoff and me to get engagements on our own again. I talked to him about it.

"What with my father, and Nan, and Nicolas, it seems that I should be where I could be called upon if necessary. If you are willing, we would refuse contracts that took us far afield".

Fortunately, Renoff understood my problems. He agreed to the suggestion, and we left the Ida Rubenstein Company, returning to Paris. We secured an engagement to dance at Olympia and in the Montmartre gymnasium resumed our practice with Paul, piecing together some of our feats and creating scenes for which Paul wrote the music.

I was still worried about Nan. One day, hearing someone refer to a pilgrimage to Lourdes, I hired a car and impulsively drove over to the Institute, suggesting we should go. Nan gave a somewhat lethargic consent and we started off. It was very hot. Nan had on a sleeveless shirt and shorts, I a thin blouse with a skirt. Neither of us wore stockings.

Nearing Lourdes, we ran into a strange convoy of vehicles, interspersed with pilgrims who walked, hobbled, limped or dragged themselves along beside the hedges. I manoeuvred the car into the procession and we moved forward inch by inch, the heat pouring down on us so that we streamed with perspiration. At this pace, we could converse with those around us, and I learned to my horror that we would have to obtain entrance tickets which were likely to be refused us because we were insufficiently covered.

"You could buy some newspapers and cover yourselves", someone suggested jokingly.

To me it was no joke. Having brought Nan all this way, I could not face disappointment. I bought several newspapers and we tied the double-sheets around our legs and arms with string.

When at last we stood in front of the water where people were being baptised, I was conscious of our extraordinary appearance, but we knelt and prayed with the rest and no one made any objections.

As we drove back to the Institute, Nan was cheerful and spoke of the future with more hope. Though no miracle had occurred, I felt that the experience had done us both good and that it had been worth the worry and the effort.

Paul came to the studio next day when I was having my ballet lesson with Nicolas, and we began talking about what we had been doing at the gymnasium. Nicolas was inclined to scoff at first, and then he said he would like Saulnier and Renoff to come over so that we could give him a demonstration.

It was a good thing he had not asked before! We had learned each feat slowly and cautiously, with Saulnier standing ready to break a fall or steady one of my partners. Now we were able to perform the act with an appearance of ease, but even so, Nicolas hovered, anxious and tense, as Renoff lifted me high on his outstretched arm and flung me towards Paul who had to catch me gracefully at the last possible moment. When it was over Nicolas wiped his forehead.

"It's certainly – spectacular", he said. "We're going to form a trio and get engagements", I told him boldly.

He protested, of course, but gradually became resigned to our folly. Soon afterwards, I received an offer for us to appear in a touring revue in England under a Russian producer with whom I had worked at one time.

We talked it over seriously but all four of us agreed that Paul, who had never even been on a stage, should make his debut in some out-of-the-way place where neither Renoff nor I would be known.

Renoff duly arranged a short engagement at Liege, in Belgium. In the first half of the programme we were to do a Spanish dance, in the second, an acrobatic extravagance called "Le Jardin Exotique". In this I was the Papillon Fantasque flying in the garden of Le Prince (Renoff). Caught in a net by the gardener (Paul) I was released and changed into a princess with whom both men fell in love, with such disastrous consequences that I changed into a butterfly again and disappeared among the roses.

When we went to the theatre for rehearsal we were confident regarding the Spanish Dance, but Paul Dukaine – as he was billed – was anxious to see what the orchestra would make of the music he had composed specially for "Le Jardin Exotique". We soon knew the worst. The violins squeaked abominably and could not keep together, the oboe was always half a bar late and the flute player stared, open-mouthed, at the score. They argued among themselves and with the conductor. Then an ultimatum was made. They would not – or they could not – play Paul's music. It must be changed!

We had practised with that music until we were dizzy. For Renoff and myself a change might not be so bad – we were used to improvisation if necessary – but for Paul it might be disastrous. However, something had to be done. We found that the orchestra could play the Spanish Dance fairly, and that they were at their best with something familiar. Paul and I spent a grueling time with the conductor and pianist piecing together extracts from their repertoire.

During the performance, I could hear Renoff muttering directions to Paul, but otherwise he came through splendidly. I do not think anyone in the audience was able to detect our difficulty and as the two

Spanish Dance

men rivals seized me by my arms and legs and whirled me around in the air like a wheel, a great storm of clapping broke out. We had made a hit!

We went back to Paris in good heart, bearing the reports of our performance at Liege. Now my Russian producer-friend was more than ever anxious to include "Le Jardin Exotique" in his revue and we agreed to join him in England.

Latterly the Paris studio had been facing great difficulties. Shop premises and showrooms in the district were now in greater demand than ever, and because the owners knew they could get an even higher rent if we vacated, ours was raised out of all proportion to profits in an attempt to drive us out.

Nicolas had heard from some of his pupils that English people's interest in ballet had increased. I promised to find out if this was true and if so to explore the possibilities of opening a studio in London again.

Before I left for England I arranged for my parents' removal to another villa; this time to Bois Colombe, on the outskirts of Paris. My father was very ill now and as I planned to fly over for frequent visits to him and to Nan, it would be as well for them to be within easier travelling distance.

"Le Jardin Exotique" had been set to new music by Paul, as we did not wish to try our orchestra too far. The three of us joined the revue "Crazy Caravan" on a roving tour. The production in general was a failure and, with inexperience, the small capital at the management's command came more quickly to an end than it would have done in capable hands.

Renoff and Paul were inclined to abandon the whole idea of the trio, but I pointed out that in both our attempts the number had attracted attention and praise. While we were still arguing about it and wondering what was the best thing to do, Walter Parnell came forward with an offer to feature us in several items in a new revue

Smoke and Flame

called "Beauty on Parade". We entered into this idea with enthusiasm. Nicolas created a delightful romantic ballet called "The Shadow of a Rose", and "Le Jardin Exotique" was completely transformed. Now the rivalry was between Chimney Sweep and Smoke, each trying to possess Flame for himself. The rooftop scenery for this acrobatic number was designed and painted by M. Albo (who had so successfully sculpted the bust of Nicolas in Paris) and the musical direction was in the hands of Vladimir Launitz. "Beauty on Parade" toured the country successfully for fifty-six weeks and critics spoke of it as "artistic and beautiful".

Our acrobatic work in "Revels of Smoke and Flame" created special attention and there were always audible gasps from the audience when I, as Flame, was tossed high in the air between my two partners. Other members of the company would crowd into the wings to watch, and one of them referred to me as "The Mighty Atom"; a nickname which stuck to me for the rest of the tour.

I was enjoying myself. The technique of this new kind of dancing came as a perpetual challenge and I delighted in making daring additions to the act. When I braced myself between Renoff and Paul and prepared for my battle with gravity, it was as though life held a new concept of beauty and power. Sometimes more conventional dancers spoke disparagingly of acrobatics and asked me if I did not miss the classical ballet for which I had been trained. I stared at them in amazement.

"How can I miss it when I have it still – but with something added?" I protested. "I learned the most difficult steps in ballet and perform them now, but I also discipline my mind and body to respond to further demands…"

To Renoff the act was a means to a living, but Paul shared my views, as well as being interested in other cults and philosophies. When we were on tour we often argued far into the night, forgetting the time until Renoff, yawning in boredom, would say, "It's almost two o'clock. I'm off to bed".

Albo, Legat, Nicolaeva, Keith Lester and Renoff

We bought a specially constructed Buick, and with Renoff driving could escape travelling by train with the rest of the company; not that we were unfriendly, but it was pleasanter this way. We played in towns all over England, and in May 1930, found ourselves in Hull as part of the hometown celebrations in honour of Amy Johnson's flight to Australia. It was all rather amusing. In the second half of the programme the curtain rose to reveal the Lord Mayor and Mr. and Mrs. Johnson, flanked by the entire company singing "Rule Britannia" and the National Anthem, while a Moth airplane, lent for the occasion, descended shakily from the flies! Paul was embarrassed because someone had revealed his identity and he was forced to make a speech.

Meanwhile Nicolas had closed the Paris studio. Between performances I was making enquiries regarding another or hopping over by air to France on a visit to my father or Nan. I found premises in Colet Gardens, near Baron's Court station, and arranged for them to be cleaned and redecorated. With its high roof, spacious floor and large windows it became one of the best studios in London; a fine stage was built so that we could give our own shows there.

In the meantime, I suggested to Nicolas that he might come over at once and begin giving lessons at the rehearsal rooms in Poland Street.

Nicolas Legat Teaching

Nicolas was not at all pleased with the Poland Street rooms. He would interrupt a lesson to shake his head and tell pupils, "Grubbee. Wait – you will see my new studio. All clean".

Here in England Nicolas was again much more noticeably foreign than he was in Paris. French he knew well, but English beat him and he never learned more than a few phrases.

But the Maestro had lost none of his teaching art. He was vehemently against regimentation and deplored other methods, which gave the same exercises over and over again; referring to this with a distasteful gesture as "the menu". He believed that pupils should develop individually along their own lines, but they had to be alert to take a new command or perform an impromptu enchainment. He had infinite patience with those who were dedicated, and with just a word or a gesture could show them how they went wrong.

"Not like Chreest", he told his class once, his arms raised sideways, his head drooped. There was no irreverence in the attitude, only a mimed revelation of beauty and sorrow…

The autumn of this year saw the first performance of the Carmargo Society. This society took its name from the great eighteenth-century dancer who insisted on shorter skirts, therefore liberating movement and throwing the way open for the development of new steps; it had nothing to do with Diaghilev,

Ninette de Valois

as some thought, and was in no way intended to revive his company, though many of its members were the first to join. For most people it seemed like the birth of British ballet.

That first Carmargo Society programme, on October 19th, closed with "Variations and Coda" produced by Nicolas Legat. The music was by Glinka and the dancing included a pas de deux by Ninette de Valois and Anton Dolin, and a Finale for the entire company. A subscription-audience of ballet enthusiasts watched the performance. I watched it, too, but must confess I could not wholly approve; some of the dancers showed a sad lack of good training.

The second Carmargo performance was held at the Cambridge Theatre on the evenings of January 25th and 26th. Nicolas arranged "Le Roi s'amuse", while Ninette de Valois contributed "Cephalus and Procris". Two days before had come the sad news of Pavlova's death at The Hague. During the performance, the lights were lowered and, to the familiar music by Saint-Saens – which for me, also, holds many memories – a spotlight played upon the empty stage. The audience stood, mourning in silent grief...

All this time I was continuing my own part in "Beauty on Parade", while on the other side of the English Channel my father's life was drawing to its close. As he became weaker, I used to fly over to see him almost daily, returning to dance in the show that same evening. One day, when I was flying in a French plane, we landed at Lympne with engine trouble. Frantic over the delay because I knew this might be the last chance of seeing my beloved father alive, I begged the authorities to make some emergency arrangements. The airport signaled to plane after plane to pick me up, and eventually I went on in an English aircraft – only to arrive too late…

I had to leave my mother and family and go back. It needed all my reserves of discipline to hide my sorrow from the audience and go through the performance as usual.

My mother came to England, and now – at last – Nan was able to join her. I wanted so much for her to be happy, but in spite of her cure, she went through a long fit of despondency. She could not dance. There was nothing else she wanted to do, and she did not care what happened to her.

Nicolas was the only one able to cheer her. His simple outlook on life seemed to fit her present need better than any deeper philosophy. "So, you cannot dance" he told her once. "There are other ways to be happy. In this mood I cannot touch you but remember – one hundred years ago you were not worried by anything; in one hundred years hence, it will be just the same. Why waste the time you are here?"

Nan suddenly told herself that what she wanted was a new interest. She loved music and knew theory and harmony, now she determined to play the piano accordion. Doctors told her it would be a mistake; that after the recent trouble with her back she should not carry so heavy an instrument, but Nan would not submit to this ruling. Now, when at last there was something she wanted to do, she would not be deprived. "Even if I die, I must take the risk", she declared dramatically.

It was not difficult for me to understand her attitude. I took risks myself. But it is always different when it is someone else; someone you love. However, Nan learned to play the accordion and it did her no harm. She took various engagements, among them one with Gypsy Petrulengro, with whose company she travelled throughout England, living in caravans. Once I found a picture of her on the front page of a daily newspaper, leading a procession, but when I enquired, Nan had only the vaguest ideas regarding its object. "I was hired only to play", she said.

During all the time I had performed in "Beauty on Parade" I had never considered an accident to myself. But one evening, when we were playing a Glasgow theatre, a careless scene shifter neglected to move from the flies a wooden shaft that had been in use for a previous turn. In my flame-coloured draperies, I twirled elusively between "Smoke" and "Sweep", each trying to secure me for their own. Now I leaped into Renoff's arms, swinging towards Paul and back again. The spectacular moment came, and the two men tossed me upwards. Too late they saw the protruding flat and I hit the stout plywood with a force that stunned me. Falling heavily into the footlights, the next thing I knew was a workman in overalls by my side, offering a glass of water. Unaware that the curtain had already been lowered, I stared at him in horror. "What are you doing here?" I whispered fiercely. "Get off the stage at once!"

With the shock of his appearance, I regained full consciousness and realised what must have happened. Staggering to my feet, I declared myself ready to go on. Renoff and Paul argued against it, but I insisted. The curtain was raised again, and I completed the act to the sound of great applause. When the doctor made his examination, however, it was found that I had sustained an injury to my knee. We were almost due to be transferred to the West End and I hated to let my partners down. Scorning the idea of rest, I performed for two nights more; then no amount of mind over matter could disguise or defeat the continual pain. "You must not go on", said Renoff. "Be sensible", urged Paul. "There is a limit to what our minds can do. Injury to bones is something you cannot control".

I could not get over the feeling that it *could* have been controlled if only I were stronger-willed. With a bad grace, I gave in, and departed for home. Now it was for me to curb my restless impatience, as I had counselled Nan to do. I had not realised it would be so hard.

Nicolaeva with Renoff and Paul Dukes

Nicolaeva and Renoff

CHAPTER FIFTEEN

Though I could not dance, I could still teach. Many already-famous dancers were again coming to the London Studio to join in with the class, or to have private lessons. The fact that so many teachers claim one pupil is puzzling until one understands that a dancer will put in an appearance at some studio for a while, then disappear on a professional engagement, to return or not as he or she feels inclined. It is up to the pupil to decide to whom they owe the most.

Sometimes there is a particular reason for a dancer's return; as when Markova took private lessons from Nicolas in preparation for the three-act "Swan Lake" at Covent Garden. She had great admiration for his teaching and once, when someone commented on the fact that he rarely demonstrated a step, she tapped her forehead and said: "He makes you think *with* him. He makes you bring the steps out of *yourself*".

Pavlova, even at the height of her fame, had still come to Nicolas for lessons, sweeping into the studio to kiss him heartily and say:

"Now, Maestro, you must please correct all my movements and show me my worst faults. I need a fresh impetus".

Besides the many famous dancers connected with the Diaghilev company, the names of Harold Turner, Pearl Argyle, Mona Inglesby, Anthony Tudor, Margot Fonteyn (as Peggy Hookham) – to mention only a few

– can be seen in the Legat register of pupils. A famous French dancer has been quoted as saying: "Whether you wish to dance with this person or that, or in this way or that, you must in the beginnings follow the precepts of a Cecchetti or a Legat".

A critic once remarked to Nicolas that one of his well-known pupils was less an artist than a technician. My husband nodded and swept an eloquent hand towards himself – then upwards: "<u>I</u> make technique", he said "*God* give artist".

Through all his years of exile from Russia, and the illness that was already overtaking him, Nicolas had never lost his sense of fun, or his skill as a cartoonist. I remember that he drew a picture of three well-known ballet critics and dubbed it "The Unholy Three". When it was published in a periodical I held my breath; in fairness it must be said that only one of the men was seriously annoyed.

THE UNHOLY TRINITY OF THE CAMARGO SOCIETY

For Nicolas, drawing was never for Art's sake alone. When a lady acquaintance begged him to make a picture of her, he answered seriously:

"Madame – I cannot draw beauty. And you are too nice".

Misunderstandings were sometimes caused by language difficulties. Knowing this, I chided him for not making more effort to learn English, and I was puzzled when, at a party, an old gentleman came across to me and remarked: "I have been having *such* an interesting conversation with your husband".

Later, repeating this remark to Nicolas, I added curiously: "How did you manage it, Kolia?"

He chuckled. "Oh, I just let him talk. Every now and then I nodded my head and said 'Aha !' That was quite enough!"

Now, at this time of enforced inactivity, I was able to pick up the threads of family life and friendships.

We still had regular news from Romola Nijinsky regarding Vaslav; their daughter, Kyra, was now our pupil. She had talent and later danced in Cochran's revues and with Reinhardt in Berlin. Had it not been for an early marriage, she might have gone farther.

Romola wrote now that Vaslav's pictures and notes were to be made into a book. She was indignant because there had been some criticism of such a move.

"Surely", she said, "if the sale of such a book enables him to have extra comforts it will be worth it?"

I could not disagree. Yet my mind went back to the

times I had seen Nijinsky dancing so brilliantly on the Maryinsky stage. The crazy pictures and the writing which were the products of his now-disordered mind could do nothing like that for Art, whatever they did to help finances.

When my knee was better, I left England for a short holiday in the South of France. Paul was staying with Renoff at his home in Nice, and I went there first, to talk over the future of the trio. When I arrived, however, it was to learn that Paul had received an invitation to visit America and wanted to accept.

"You will easily find someone to take my place", he said.

I was sorry to lose such a sympathetic partner – Paul was one of the few people with whom I was able to discuss the philosophies and creeds which interested me so much – but I never expected that dancing would hold him for long.

Renoff had temporarily taken up film work, and in any case I could make no further decisions regarding our future partnership until I had discussed this new development with Nicolas. I settled down to enjoy the rest of my short stay.

I discovered two more unusual people to add to my collection; Doctor Lacour, a French homeopathist who baked bread which he exposed to the sun's rays believing it to be thus impregnated with health-giving properties, and an Egyptian called Hassan who lived the life of a hermit and cured people with herbs and hypnotism. He was also a masseur, and his magical touch completed the cure of my knee.

Renoff and I returned to England together and asked Nicolas for his advice about our next move. I was half inclined to take Paul's defection as a pointer and settle down to teaching only, but Nicolas urged me to go on with stage

Lydia Kyasht in "Javotte" arr. by Nicolas Legat

work, saying: "I have always told you that I am too old for you, but it was never my intention to make you match me. Dancing is your life".

It was Nicolas who suggested Keith Lester might take Paul's place. Keith was a young man of Scottish descent who started dancing with Anton Dolin and continued with lessons from Nicolas. He partnered Lydia Kyasht for two years, and Karsavina for three. Now he was studying again at the studio.

Keith was attracted to acrobatic dancing and agreed to complete the trio. We joined "Beauty on Parade" again, touring the country once more with success. Then Renoff began to suffer from stomach trouble and doctors decided he must take a rest.

I formed my own little company, and Keith and I worked together on some new numbers *a deux*, presenting the show in many French towns. Keith was a breezy personality and fun to work or play with. Off-stage, he liked to wear the kilt and his splendid but unusual appearance created an interest that was sometimes embarrassing. I remember once, as he and I walked along the promenade at Marseilles – he in his kilt and I in my beach-pajamas – a little crowd followed to laugh and exclaim: *"Regardez bien! Monsieur a mit le jupon, et Madame son pantalon!"*

Another memory was of a dance when I wore a new white dress with gold embroidery around the hem. As Keith lifted me high above his head, a sharp end of thread nicked his eyebrow. The wound was superficial, but for some reason the blood poured from it, running down his face, staining my dress, dripping on to his own costume. I had no idea what had happened, and we carried on with the dance to the end, but I was terribly worried, thinking his eye to be badly cut. The audience loved it, of course, and clapped Keith's gallantry with enthusiasm. We laughed at the tiny scratch afterwards, but I was rather sad about the ruin of my lovely dress!

During part of this tour we had with us the two children of Bronislava Nijinska; she was going to Buenos Aires, and left in my charge Irena, a girl of about fifteen, and Leva, who was twelve.

Keith Lester, Renoff and Nicolaeva

Leva had wanted to take ballet lessons from me, and though his talent was music rather than dancing, he became my devoted admirer and worked as he had done for no one before. He was a little like his uncle in appearance, with the same type of shy personality.

Later, when the children rejoined their family in Paris, came tragedy. Returning from a thanksgiving service to Sainte Terese, the car in which they were driving skidded, and young Leva was killed outright. Not until almost a year later could his mother bear to open the small case the boy had taken with him on this last journey. Then she found in it a diary in which was written: "I have not always been in school when my mother thought I was. Instead, I walked through fields and woods. I feel I must make the most of my time, for it seems to me that I may not have long to live..." It seemed hard that this family should suffer another great blow...

With Nan

When the tour with Keith ended, I spent a few days with Nan, now living in Paris. She was having some gay times, but she had not yet found real happiness. I suggested she should come back to England, and she promised to think it over.

Back in London, I thought Nicolas did not seem well. He coughed a great deal and had lost much of his splendid energy. When I seemed concerned, he declared there was nothing more than usual wrong, and that in any case he was being treated by an Armenian doctor in whom he had great faith. I tried to persuade him not to smoke so much, and carted back pints of milk from the nearby dairy, insisting he should drink it. "Don't fuss", he said.

We had a new pupil from Yugoslavia. Self-taught, Ana Roje had danced in her own country and created such a good impression that the Government granted her a scholarship and sent her to England to study with Nicolas. Her boyish appearance and affection for both of us made her refer to herself laughingly as "your son" and indeed, she soon became as one of the family. Her knowledge of Russian and English was slight, but she was quick to learn and was soon demonstrating the Legat method to other

Ana Roje
Photo courtesy of Tasha Betram

pupils.

When Renoff came over to England we were offered another tour, and Nicolas urged us to accept. When I told him that I thought I should not leave him again he became quite angry; the fear that he might become a brake on my career was now almost an obsession.

"You <u>must</u> he insisted". Then he put his hand on my shoulder and smiled. "Once I thought of you and Nan as my wife and daughter. Now it sometimes seems to me that you are both my daughters--".

Before I made the final decision we talked it over with Ana. Nicolas said: "I have taught my wife all I know, and I am confident that when I am gone she will uphold my methods in this country. Meanwhile, I should like you to help me".

Ana agreed to live in the house while I was away and to do all she could for Nicolas. My brother-in-law would be in charge of the business side, as before.

I should not be away long, I told myself.

The tour on which Renoff and I had embarked was successful, and we were asked to extend it; which we did, in view of reassuring letters from home. Ana sent satisfactory reports on the work at the Studio, and on Nicolas's health; he, himself, wrote cheerfully. There was good news too, from Nan who had met a man she loved and was going to marry him.

Renoff and I were dancing in Bucharest when a telegram came saying Nicolas had been suddenly taken ill with pneumonia. We came straight home.

Before we arrived, pleurisy had set in, and at the crisis death was very near. Nicolas, however, recovered, and when he was at last convalescent, I urged him to go for a holiday with my sister and her husband.

"They are off to Germany", I told him. "And Olga Preobrajanskaya is at Bad Mundster – you have often said you would like to see her again".

The holiday and the change seemed to revive Nicolas completely. Delighted to meet again his former pupil and partner, he sent back lively and amusing letters containing snapshots of the reunion.

The improvement proved only temporary. On his return, his appearances at the studio were infrequent, and he came only to watch, sitting quietly beside me as if aware that the treasured "tradition" was safe in my hands.

Pupils from Flora Fairburn's School came once a week to the Studio for class lessons. Among them was a red haired, freckled ten-year-old called Moira King, who afterwards became famous as Moira Shearer. Born in Scotland, she had been with her parents in Rhodesia where she studied under a Russian teacher, then came back to England to attend the Fairburn School. Soon I was giving her two lessons a week.

The brunt of the teaching fell now on me, for Ana Roje, who had looked after Nicolas so faithfully while I was away, was now engaged to Oscar Harmos – another dancer from Yugoslavia – who had followed her to England.

Towards the end of 1936 there seemed such a deterioration in Nicolas's health that I persuaded him to have another check-up at St. Mary's hospital. To him, they gave a reassuring report; but to me they told the truth. His lungs were so badly affected that they could do nothing for him. I had scarcely rallied from this shock when Ana Roje and Oscar Harmos were offered an engagement to dance together; I could not stand in their way and said goodbye to them.

Ana was in tears. "You will be all right? I hate leaving you here alone".

"Don't worry, Son", I said, trying to smile.

All my time was spent now in looking after my husband and filling his place in the studio. We had a party there on January the 13th, for the Russian New Year, but Nicolas was not well enough to put in an appearance. Serge Renoff offered to come and help me keep his old Maestro company and finding the crisis near, stayed to see it through. He lay on the floor outside the bedroom those last few nights, so that I could call him at once –

Nicolas Legat died on January 24th, 1937. For me it was more than the loss of a husband. My relationship with this fine, sensitive man had woven a golden thread through my life, even in childhood. He was my Maestro and I attributed all I knew of dancing to his method, my advanced technique to his patient correction and advice.

Many people now paid tribute to him. Among others published was that of Pearl Argyle of the Vic-Wells ballet, who wrote in "The Dancing Times", "Nicolas Legat never complained, was never bad-tempered. One *enjoyed* his classes. His *enchainements* were dances in themselves".

The London Times spoke of the Studio at Colet Gardens as "a centre of artistic life" and added "Nicolas Legat served his art implicitly all through his life, though it often happened that his work was known to the world at large only through the exquisite performances of his pupils…"

Perhaps Nicolas himself put it best in the closing passage of his book "Ballet Russe". He wrote: "In the four quarters of the globe I behold the greatest dancers of my generation, many of them my pupils, upholding the standard of this great Art. If I am proud at the sight it is not merely a personal pride, but a national pride. We shall live forever in thus transmitting the otherwise inexpressible soul of Russia. With this ideal I live, and with his ideal untarnished, I shall die…"

CHAPTER SIXTEEN

My own dancing career had come to an end. It was my husband's wish that I should carry on the great tradition he stood for, and this I now determined to do.

An immediate problem was that of teaching to suitable music. Nicolas always accompanied his classes; in early days with his violin and afterwards improvising at the piano. To him this seemed the only satisfactory way of getting the spontaneity which was such a feature of this method. I had learned the piano as a child, but I had not played for years.

My earnest desire to be a faithful disciple made me impatient with pianists who could play only to a standard rhythm and were not able to adjust themselves to unexpected demands. I felt that if only I could solve this question satisfactorily, I would be able to give closer attention to the teaching itself.

Dismissing the pianist, I tried beating out the time with a stick and singing a melody to go with it. But the strain of combining this with dancing directions resulted in a temporary loss of my voice and I was forced to try something else. For a time, I thought castanets were the answer, but they do not give the full tone needed for adagio work.

Almost in despair, I sat down at the piano one day facing my class, my hands resting on the keys. My mind struggled across the unknown void in a wordless appeal to the man whose spirit I felt myself dedicated to perpetuate.

To my surprise and joy my fingers found the right notes to form a pleasant, if undistinguished melody. I played on, not looking at my hands but at my pupils and the music continued to take care of itself. From that moment I was able to accompany my classes, fitting the rhythm to the movement of the dancers as they responded to my commands.

This new-found ability was a great asset. The musical part of my dancing had always held significance, but I agreed with Nicolas's view that it should always be subordinate to interpretation. We had found all the best musicians

Photo Courtesy Legat Foundation

to be of the same opinion. In Russia, Nicolas once approached the great composer, Tcherepnine, telling him that I was finding difficulty with a dancing phrase which came into the opera "Dobrinya Nikitisch".

"It is a beautiful variation", he said, "but the music does not allow time for the steps to be performed to perfection. Could you slow it down a little there?"

"But of course," Tcherepnine replied. "It is for you

and Nicolaeva to decide. To bring out a dancer's individuality there should always be partnership between the performer and the music".

The studio continued to grow, and many pupils who had studied exclusively with Nicolas before his death, now remarked on the similarity of our teaching, yet surely this was no wonder. For very many years Nicolas and I had been teacher and pupil, as well as man and wife.

Early in 1938, we had another New Year's party at the Studio, with two hundred people present. Moira King (Shearer) danced the doll to Barbara Vernon's Coppelius.

In the same year, I wrote eight articles on Russian Folk Dances for the "Dancing Times" and began to gather the notes on ballet-technique which Nicolas and I had long planned to make into a book. (*Subsequently published as "Ballet Education" in 1947 by Duckworth & Co.*)

In July, the Russian Ballet Association was formed, and the inaugural meeting was held at the studio. Those interested included members of the old Russian Imperial Family who watched the show, and we had the sympathetic approval of Mesdames Kschesinskaya, Prebrajanskaya and Kyasht, as well as that of Oboukhoff, Anton Dolin and many others.

One of the people who became interested in my work was John Masefield, the poet Laureate. He came to the studio one day with his wife, at the invitation of Margaret Severn, one of my older students. Absorbed in the lesson, I did not take much notice of the distinguished looking, grey haired visitor, but when afterwards he professed himself fascinated by what he had seen and asked to come again, we became friendly.

Moira Shearer
Photo Courtesy of
Tasha Betram

He invited me to arrange some ballets for the Oxford Festival. Patricia Ryan, who later became head of the Irish Ballet School which I was asked to found, Moira Shearer, who had continued with me and become a full-time pupil in this her third and final year, and Barbara Vernon, who won the World Championship in Paris in the Autumn; these three were among the pupils who took part in the programme. The evening was an unqualified success and at its close, in recognition of the work I had put into the occasion John Masefield presented me with a beautiful edition of the book "Tribute to Ballet", signed by him, personally.

He also read an ode of his own composition, from which I quote this extract:

"Last, it remains to call a cheer
On Madame Nadine Legat here.

She, once the Russian Ballet's Queen,
Wonder and glory of the scene,
Now teaches, that the Art she served
May flower here and be preserved.
We say to her: 'Be soon returning
To this grey city full of learning,
And take with thanks, from Thames' Valley
A writer's tribute to THE BALLET'."

Among serious students of dancing, I think I have a reputation for patience and enthusiasm, but I find it difficult to tolerate amateurishness. When I was asked to adjudicate at a Festival in Blackpool, I did not relish the idea and not only put my services at a high price, but also asked for accommodation for my mother, two Pekinese dogs, and myself. I thought that would be the end of it, but the sponsors agreed to my conditions and I had to attend.

I was horrified by the low standard of dancing. Child after child appeared on the platform to sing the same song, tummies protruding horridly as they tap-danced; or what was almost worse, they performed "ballet" steps, their toes scratching like chickens. I was bored almost to tears, and after a heavy lunch supplied by a generous management, had difficulty in even keeping my eyes open. Once I did drift into a doze and was nudged awake by my next door neighbour. "You must not sleep, dear Madame", she whispered reprovingly. "The mothers of the children will complain that the judging was unfair…"

I pulled myself together, but for long afterwards I remembered the ordeal in that oft-repeated ditty: "I shall dance my way to heaven…" I even wrote an article about it!

Nan was married the following year and I was happy about it. Their marriage remains a good partnership still.

In the late summer of 1939, war was again threatening everyone's happiness. People expected London to be the first target and the families of many of my pupils began to be apprehensive. Moira King was evacuated to Scotland, and other children departed to various parts of the country. It seemed likely that the studio was in for a lean time, and with my mother's safety in mind, I toyed seriously with the idea of evacuation. Massine, whose ballet-company I had been coaching, was off to America and begged me to come too. But this I would not do. I did, however, contemplate removing to what might be considered a safer part of the country.

The idea strengthened as one after another of the parents came to me, asking what they should do about their children. By the time I had made up my mind to do as they wished and start a ballet school somewhere else, the possible number of evacuees had increased to thirty-six, and I began to feel like the Pied Piper.

On the day war was declared, I left London with two coaches full of people, and only the vaguest idea where to go. My sister had a little cottage in Essex which would, I thought, at least provide a halting place.

In the middle of the evening, when I was still stranded with my pupils, a young policeman came to my rescue. His home was on Mersey Island where, he said, there were many empty seaside bungalows which we should be able to rent quite cheaply.

This proved correct. With my mother and the younger children, I stayed in a small house, while the older children were variously disposed of in the bungalows.

The house became the centre of our activities; the dining room a classroom, studio, and dormitory in turn. Three times a day the furniture must be taken out into the garden or, if wet, crammed into the kitchen and the small hall while dancing classes were in progress; the room rearranged for sleeping in at night. If fine, we ate out of doors.

I hired a bicycle and cycled the two or three miles to the nearest shops to buy food, for there was but a small bus which went into the town and back once daily.

We lived thus for three months, but as the weather became colder and there was constant rain, it was obvious that some change must be made.

Someone suggested that Buckinghamshire was a safe area and leaving my large family in the charge of my mother, now Baboushka (grandmother) to all these children, I set off to find another home.

In Beaconsfield, High Wycombe, and Amersham I tramped from house agent to house agent, without success. Even unattractive properties had been quickly snapped up at the time of the crisis.

Then one morning a Beaconsfield agent told me of a house that had just become available. I went to see it and had doubts about its suitability; for one thing, it was not as large as I had hoped for. Deciding to give the matter further thought I walked to the corner for a bus which would take me back to the agent's where I could return the keys and discuss it with him.

From where I stood, I could still see the house. As I waited, a car passed it slowly, then drew up. A man got out pushed open the gate and walked through the garden, looking up at the windows. Then he came over to me and raised his hat. "Excuse me", he said politely, "I wonder if you could tell me the name of the agent for that house?" For a second I hesitated, wondering if I should hand over the keys. But they were my responsibility, and I wanted time to think, so I merely gave him the information he asked for. He thanked me, adding: "Could I give you a lift into Beaconsfield?"

I got in beside him. As we drove along, my mind was in turmoil. If I hesitated too long about the house, this man would get his offer in first; perhaps he would make one immediately – even without seeing the inside. Panic mounted as we drew nearer the town. While the man was trying to find somewhere to park the car, I excused myself and jumped out. Rushing into the agent's office I made a quick deal and left, averting my head when I caught sight of my driver crossing the street.

After all, I did see it first, I told myself. Without the definite intention, I had founded on Mersey Island the first ballet boarding school in England. The new premises were named "First House" and the re-evacuation from Essex took place.

The idea of a school where children could study dancing side by side with a general education was based on the old Imperial Schools of Russia; even the uniform I designed was similar. Other students of the ballet heard of the venture and more pupils were added. Pioneers rarely receive their due. Now this sort of school is a regular feature of student ballet education.

As the enemy blitz on London increased in fury, more and more people were added to our household, for I could not bear to turn anyone away. The bedrooms overflowed, and at night there were people sleeping in the living rooms and along the corridors; food for everyone was a continual headache. My friends maintained stoutly that I never went to bed. Certainly, I had never worked so hard. I gave ballet classes, taught French, Russian, and several other subjects; cooked, cleaned, washed the smaller children, made tutus for the pupils and nursed them when they were not well. At the same time, the school managed to put on frequent shows for charitable war efforts.

My mother, though now over eighty years of age, helped with the cooking and the welfare of the children. The tapping of her stick along the corridors of

"First House", her commands in Russian or French and the curtsies which she insisted on from the pupils were quite a feature of the regime. A distinguished Indian philosopher – Professor Varma – was another of the "unusual" people whose friendship made me proud. He lived in a hut in the garden, taught the children Yoga and massaged away their aches and pains with a magic touch. Miss Egles and her sister helped with the educational side.

In spite of the war and the difficulties of food restrictions, it was a gay community. Many people took an interest in the school's progress and helped to make it the artistic centre of the district.

As the house became more crowded, it occurred to me that the big garage would make a splendid studio and release more room inside. Workmen's services were almost unobtainable at the time, but everyone set to work with a will. The garage was cleaned and distempered, barres attached to the walls and mirrors fixed. Always impatient, I was longing to put it into use, the moment the paint had dried. But there was still the piano to move and it seemed that even with combined strength this would be a difficult task. I decided to wait until there were men around. Then I remembered – there *was* a man! According to reports he had called early in the day and refused to leave without seeing me, but I had been too busy.

Was he still here? I threw open the door of the small study off the hall and saw a huge man who seemed almost to fill the room. He burst out in a flood of Russian: "Madame Legat, I have come all the way from St. Ives in Cornwall because your friends have told me that you are here…"

I could not remember meeting anyone who had the name he gave, but foremost in my mind was the removal of the piano, and I could think of nothing but this man's providential size. I asked him into the other room and waved a careless hand towards the piano.

"I have been wondering how I could get it across to my new studio", I told him.

He threw me a confident smile and entered into the idea at once. "I, myself, shall move it for you, Madame", he said, and putting his great shoulders against the instrument, half pushed, half lifted it out of the house and across the garden with only my feeble efforts to help him.

When it was in place, he turned to me and explained simply that he wished to remain at First House. After the service he had done me, it seemed churlish to refuse, but I explained that it was quite impossible; we were overcrowded now.

The Russian shrugged and glanced round the converted studio. "Here I stay", he asserted.

I was fearful now at what I might have let myself in for, but he was certainly too big to argue with. Already he was settling himself down in a corner, and I wondered if he might not be a little mad; should I shut the doors quickly and lock him in? But that seemed rather mean.

I went back to the house and got on with my work, determined not to worry about it. The man stayed for a few days, making no trouble when we wanted him to vacate the studio, and drifting into the kitchen at the prescribed times for meals. Just as I was becoming used to considering him yet another member of my large household, he suddenly disappeared. I never saw him again.

During the four and a half years of the war, a number of parents applied for their daughters' – or sons' – entry into my ballet school, but without success. I was forced to refuse through lack of accommodation. When peace came I decided that "First House" had outlived its usefulness, and larger premises must be found.

In 1945, I again went prospecting. It was not easy to decide where to found our new home, but eventually I settled on Royal Tunbridge Wells; in Regency days a fashionable resort, now a quiet country town. Here, set on a hill in attractive though woefully neglect-

The Legat School,
Tunbridge Wells

ed grounds, I discovered the house that was to be the second "Legat School."

John Masefield, himself, wrote to me thus: "The thought of your school beginning is to me a light showing that the tide of darkness has turned.... may you find this really a time of the re-birth of beauty and grace, and countless glad young souls coming to you to know of these things".

In Tunbridge Wells, at that time, there were still prisoners of war, and I employed some of them to work in the gardens. They were, unfortunately, ignorant of such a calling, pulling up plants instead of weeds and pruning trees so drastically that they bore no fruit. To me, however, these men were individuals. When I discovered that some of them were musicians I encouraged them to form an orchestra – they proved more successful at accompanying ballet performances!

Many Russians sought us out now, eager to speak their own language and tell me hard-luck stories. I took one girl on as a maid, but she hung round the Studio door so wistfully that I soon found myself giving her ballet lessons, when she should have been cleaning rooms. Another Russian called at the school with his wife and daughter. The latter had married an English soldier who was now demobilised, and this young man talked me into making him my business manager.

For a time, it seemed that he might be right in arguing that he could save me expense and relieve me of minor jobs. But one day– alas – he disappeared without a word to his wife or her parents and I was faced with huge bills from local shops, which should have been paid!

Yes, the school has survived many crises. I feel that it was destined to exist and there were always genuine people who lent a hand in such moments; among these must be mentioned Catherine Weguelin who worships the Legat tradition. Before she came I had no reliable person to advise me, and as everyone knows, it is rare indeed for an artist to have a head for business.

Nan's husband is a linguist and all through the war he worked on Continental Intelligence. Now he was in Austria on Telephone Censorship, and Nan with him.

Doctors told her it would be unwise for her to have a child, but this was her dearest wish and now – while she could have plenty of rest – she was determined again to take a risk for something she wanted. Soon after, her little daughter, Mimi, was born. I longed to see my granddaughter, but there was no possibility of going to them. I was too busy.

Each day the pupils assembled in the early morning for the Yoga exercises which I believe control breathing, muscles, and mind. After breakfast, older students had ballet classes while the younger children struggled with the three R's. All day long the old house echoed to the sound of dancing feet, to the music of pianos, and voices counting: "And one and two and…"

A letter came from Romola Nijinsky. At long last she had obtained permission to bring Vaslav to England and they were now living in an hotel about twenty miles from London. Would I come to see him? Nijinsky had altered, of course. He was no longer the good-looking boy of the Maryinsky days, but I talked to him in Russian, reminding him of Nicolas and the Imperial School. He seemed interested and came often to see me, but when I asked him to dance, he shook his head. "I have lost the habit", he declared.

Barbara Vernon was married during the war to another dancer: John Gregory. Their little boy became my godson. When their daughter was born I wondered if it might please Vaslav if he were asked to be the child's godfather. The Gregorys were delighted, and Nijinsky came to my school where the christening was to take place. He seemed to understand the part he was to play, but when I tried to place the child in his arms he shook his head and hid behind his wife.

In 1950, he died at the London Clinic and again Romola sent for me. I went at once. As we stood looking down at Vaslav's body, Romola was beside herself with grief and cried out: "Isn't he beautiful, Nadia? Tell him so. Tell him he was a beautiful dancer".

Romola Nijinsky is now in the United States. At her request, I translated from the Russian the notes which Vaslav used when he tried to create a system of notation on the basis of the old one. With my busy life, I was unable to do more than a few pages at a time, and there were great difficulties of interpretation; but it is finished at last and has been passed over to Romola.

When Nan returned from Austria with her husband and child, they came to live in the lodge by the gates, and Nan took over the care of the younger children; Mimi grew up with them.

Many well-known people have taken an interest in the school; Sir Paul Dukes (of "Revels of Smoke and Flame" days) was one of its first Governors and he has several times employed pupils from the School in his television broadcasts and films on the subject of Yoga. Basil Dean, Anton Dolin, Ram Gopal and Violetta Elvin are among those who have distributed prizes at the annual garden party.

Now we have moved to large premises at Goudhurst. Here, girls and boys of every nationality and creed find a meeting-ground in the Art of Dancing. Here, in our entrance hall still stands the bust of Nicolas Legat from whom I inherited the great tradition of the "Russian School".

Madame Legat Teaching

A FINAL NOTE

The Albo bust of Nicolas Legat is now on loan to the Royal Ballet in Covent Garden, London and a copy has been donated by Madame Legat's granddaughter Mimi, to the Vaganova Academy in St. Petersburg, Russia.

Mimi Legat, who was trained by her grandmother at the Legat School, went on to perform with The Norwegian Ballet, The Hamburg State Opera, the Ballet Royal de Wallonie in Charleroi, Belgium, and The Washington National Opera, Washington, D.C.

Mimi Legat in "Coq d'Or"

Ms. Legat was instrumental in producing this work. She selected the photographs and other images which are mostly from the family collection.